Christopher Levenson

VIRGIN SCIENCE

Also by Pier Giorgio Di Cicco

We Are the Light Turning   *1976*
The Sad Facts   *1977*
The Circular Dark   *1977*
A Burning Patience   *1978*
Roman Candles (ed.)   *1978*
Dancing in the House of Cards   *1978*
Dolce-Amarro   *1979*
The Tough Romance   *1979*
A Straw Hat for Everything   *1981*
Flying Deeper into the Century   *1982*
Dark to Light; Reasons for Humanness   *1983*
Women We Never See Again   *1984*
Post-Sixties Nocturne   *1985*

Pier Giorgio Di Cicco

Virgin Science

hunting holistic paradigms

McCLELLAND AND STEWART

The Canadian Publishers
McClelland and Stewart Limited
481 University Avenue, Toronto M5G 2E9

Canadian Cataloguing in Publication Data

Di Cicco, Pier Giorgio, 1949–
    Virgin science

Poems.
ISBN 0-7710-2103-8

I. Title.

PS8557.I248V57 1986   C811'.54   C86-094308-9
PR9199.3.D52V57 1986

The publisher makes grateful acknowledgment to the Canada Council and the Ontario Arts Council for their financial assistance.

Set in Perpetua by The Typeworks, Vancouver
Printed and bound in Canada by T. H. Best Printing Company Limited

Some of these poems appeared, in earlier versions, in *The Canadian Forum, Arc, Poetry Toronto,* and *Poetry Canada Review,* and in the anthologies *The New Canadian Poets* (ed. Dennis Lee) and *Canadian Poetry Now* (ed. Ken Norris); some were broadcast on "State of the Arts," CBC.

This is for Fred Demanuele,
and in memory of Gastone Aguzzi

"My eternity has died, and I am waking it."
— César Vallejo

CONTENTS

I

DYING TO MYSELF

"But giving life is not so easy.
It doesn't mean handing it out to some mean fool, or
letting the living dead eat you up.
It means kindling the life-quality where it was not, . . . "
— D. H. Lawrence

"Other atmospheres depreciate, discourage, and enfeeble graciousness; for example, those of Puritan fanaticism, authoritarian bureaucracy, canny calculation, and, most hopeless of them all, that of power seeking rationally to justify itself, that mechanized inhumanity which has come to the fore in our modern era."
— Romano Guardini

"Ed è morte
uno spazio nel cuore."
— Salvatore Quasimodo

I remember him.
He used to hate evil, talked of
fighting it, resisted his eyes
that couldn't have found a sliver of
grief — he bothered himself about
hating what the world hated, just to be
kind; that was the irony of it, the
idiocy of it. He was a father

with the child inside him; and the women
shouted let the child in you come out,
as if they were talking liberation;
and what would they do with a child but
own it. Truly, the father was

not necessary and wanted to give the child
up for adoption. This father, called ego,
misguided care, a reflection of providence,

this faithless son of a bitch that remembered,
like braille, early graces, whose memory held
out more than others, who began giving away
what he didn't have left to give, except honour,

integrity, the will to live, this immolating
thing run into the altar of common need,

surrendering his faith out of love,
when all they could utter was give, give,
need, *helplessly,* need *and* give, need
and give, *in a town that confused community*
with Marxism, in a town that wanted to have
faith on its own terms —

he crumbled. I remember him, in the bed of
his own making with the blinded eyes
of good faith, because he simply
couldn't remember where to drink
and what had made him. That long ago

I give him every snowfall to come, to
cool his eyes, his hot angry eyes.
He was the father that tried for me,
whose shell I lift up, whom I will
save with my sincerity, who hangs even now
on the trees like an exhausted ghost.

These are the most beautiful times
in my life; Mario and Alfredo and the spirit
of life, the entourage always coming to
the door; the woman with her mouth flowering
into bouquets of honesty; yesterday's disasters
so distasteful to themselves they come
snivelling up to the doorstep wanting
a little bit of light; the poem spurring itself
on because hope draws the line by the teeth.
The virtues lining themselves up like street-lamps
down the avenue, at first sputtering, then making
the world sensible with daylight —
      I don't know what I want to ruminate
of the past, but the guts extend themselves
by the grace of something other.
      I have grown up to be a metaphysician —
an apple is a kiss, a friend is a smile,
and these things are not poetry —
I leave it to the post-modern to see a coded
transform for the song in their lungs.
      The visions return, after ten years
of watching faithlessness eat people out of one bed
into another. I do not wait for them to come awake.
I do not want company. I sledgehammer my
grief, without fear of repression, and it comes out
azaleas, marigolds, whatever you like —
the soul has its own tastes.
      Sentimentality is what the proud fear,
so they never get to the outrageously beautiful.
This is my only grief in a Protestant
country — they have no talent for metaphysics.
My friend Mario talks to Alfredo across the table
and describes him as a flower growing on his shoulder —

In a five mile radius they would laugh at this
In a five foot radius they would laugh at this
In a five inch radius they would laugh —
But Mario has become the hub of the world
and its circumference — two things at once —
and in Berkeley they are trying to get over
the Uncertainty Principle, how to be two things at
once, male and female, particle and anti-particle —
The Italians live with paradox as an act of faith
humbled to the ridiculous and courting the angels —
well, to be brutal about it, it isn't just the Italians
that could do this. The obedient to heart could do it.
Someday the scientists will localize pride in
the Protestant brain, and we will be having
a good laugh at this, and we won't say a thing —
we will have evolved into something other than a concept —
perhaps as a smile behind a tree, a poem, a song,
an old photo of the family in Molise — into the
unlikeliest thing, the way God makes something out
of nothing, under the quantum quiffs,
knowing that poetry is science wise enough to know
that you have to live with your metaphors.
        But, as it stands, this is the most beautiful
time in my life. When I am out of grace, I will
forget it, and you will see me long-faced, on Bloor,
discussing Kafka, and Germaine Greer and systems
holism. I would thank God, if he weren't so busy with
me, so I will thank Mario and the other angels —
There is one more apologia, every time I
forget to say *thank you;* and it occurs to me
grazie means thanks in Italian, while
the English say you're welcome, when they mean goodbye.

I am a success.
Everyone I love is alive,
undiseased, doing moderately well, or
splendidly well. The temperature has shot
up ten degrees in February and it feels like April.
The baby next door has clammed up.
The lights are skittering, and what
could be better than like this to be in the
pink, in the correct flesh pour moi and loving
like a lifeline all those I love. Even the
American Secretary of State is asleep.
He can't get out of hand while he's asleep.
Reagan's sneaking to his kitchen, cramming
jelly beans down his throat. They're distracted,
all's right with the world, so let's make love, let's
commemorate years, let's look ahead and let the future
balance the gifts of the past. It's a moment of
cosmic reprieve and I want to live forever. A moment
more and I'll go happily. Things are glowing,
lamps, books, bits of the room begin a soft glow,
shaking hands with each other. I can even think
fondly of Ethel Merman, whose voice makes me puke,
and Ted Shirey who let me think he'd died in Vietnam —
to have come so far and feeling this good I am
lying down in fields, baseball diamonds, parking lots,
face up to the sun, affording to remember good times.
I remember the look of that damned sun, and it is
like sun in this room tonight — feeling that good
to myself.
        There isn't that much more to it.
Why don't you come in? a Human in each other's
lives, a carnival wheel of flesh and thought

and the heart coming up lucky.

    Did you get a Valentine's card from me this
year. Oh well, I meant to send it. How is your
serenity in 1994? What about El Salvador? This is
any will to change, where the good starts, in this
courage to be arbitrary, this feeling, this nod at
life ce soir. Tomorrow morning, we bleed freshly,
separately, standing on the shoulders of a kiss.
But tonight, feeling damned good, that's the ticket,
that's the thing, the only idea you'll ever have
in your life; you will recognize it, like a number
on your wrist, any year from now, the brand of sun,
the mark of a man who was successful in something,
anything, at home in the world for a night.

I feel good here.
The words resound, like apex from
the heart, or like a second skin
forgotten, like a dead brother
one had failed to light candles for;
like dawn coming in off the left
flank of the planet, pale with a mouthful
of old promises and you leave the back door
open to let it in. You sit in the armchair
and you feign nonchalance, while morning becomes
beautiful with the mantle flowers; ah, how you
always loved a change of heart better than
a change of scene, but this world calls for
travelling now. You come back to places of
happiness like land claimed from the sea
and you irrigate it with heart hoping for some
of the old verdure from the time of Atlantis
when you swam with your friends through
the portals of symmetry, one flesh
reflecting another; it is colder upstairs
on the shingles of earth where you
grow platonic shadows like coffins out of which
azaleas astonish the eyes, memorial and
salutary. This time they transmute into
streetcar tracks ribboning laser on the
lovely curve of a village in the city. It is
a pinnacle of distress and vigil, a Venice
hoisted above mundaneness and wasp acumen.
The sky tears into an ochre out of which
clouds loll like restless hills. It is the
involutions of prayer that the sky makes,
like words drawn from a boy as he looks out
an attic window before he learns to talk,

before he stammers into stunned gratitude
with words like *I feel good here*. What has he done
to return a prayer, what kind of exhaustion
with the world in his lungs as he pulls out
of Atlantis onto the altar of evolution
with tired words like a rib, like a lump
of clay out of which he will fashion some
Galatea, some creature with leaves for hands.
Any analogy would do; it is a homesteader's voice,
joy beaten to instinct as he finds his plot of
ground. *I feel good here*. It is a sound that
looks like innocence when all illusions are shot.
There are the anonymous even in Heaven,
and the spirit with which they arrive
doesn't deter anything; it is the inconspicuous
brushing of angels' gowns, or just the way
a man walks down an avenue, jostling the
sound of children.

These are the most extraordinary women in the world,
they do not go to bed at 11 p.m.
when they dance, they dance with you,
when they sing, it is the motherhood of half the world,
when they go walking, they have an affair with sunlight;
these are the women that hold men's faces in the palm of
their hands, these are the women that men go back to, because
they do not come easy and they do not come hard. These women
are poetry. They arrange for their sons and daughters the
minute they see the sun, because the sun is a beautiful thing
to sit under. To love the air is to want to fill it with lovers.

These women do not understand words like
would, likely, depending —
there are english words
that have no place in the mouths of people,
there are words made up for the language of thought,
that have forgotten to serve the language of lovers.
These words are in a manual at the bottom of the ocean,
where strange fish gnaw upon them,
uncomprehending fish that mouth the strange words
like *relationship, perhaps, except, attachment.*
The most extraodinary women in the world,
above, are sunning on beaches; when they sigh,
trees far off are heard breathing in
the loveliest towns in the world.

I've been looking at your photograph all day;
and it's amazing, it looks just like you,
almost moving — I can see your eyes squint into
that seriousness, that small mouth blow wisps
of cigarette smoke; those teeth underpinning
laughter. It won't mean much to anyone but me.
You never do, mean much to anyone but me.
You did not matter before me, not the way you
are to me. No one made much of you, not before me.
I make a lot out of you. The moon! nah, that's
not enough, I make clothes for souls out of you
and wrap them round my friends, and it keeps them
warm; *what are you wearing,* they ask my
friends and they reply — a bit of love Giorgio
made out of this woman. There was enough lovin'
to go around, it keeps the neighbourhood warm, the town —
it's big news! this fellow loves, and trees glow
after sunlight on them — an extra shine; the clarity
of robins singing, have you noticed it lately?
Water has a luminescence. You send all this
from a thousand miles away and it's the chief export
of the planet right now. It's been Earth's major
export for three thousand years — they know it in
the galaxy; it's what keeps the sun revolving around
the child in the park; sweet ignoramuses, that's
what we are.
Your photograph is like a satellite in the planet,
reflecting love to the solar system; what did
you think kept things up? Gravity? What physics? There
is no particle of matter smaller than the heart.
Nothing mattered before you; you did not matter before me.
They say *why do you stare at that photograph*
day in and day out? It is where the earth folds in,

it is holography, it is a black hole between
portraits and windows that breaks into a white
hole where we trip into an innocence — the way we
were in every minute that we're in; beautiful,
a doppleganger, made possible by love. It is the
laser, this photograph that floats the hologram of
leaves and streets and people.
It is such an excellent photograph.
I can almost see you smiling, almost pleased
with the inventions of love.
Smile, damn you, come into the room like
a creator, with your hair down.

I love these boys.
They have such small, limber souls
that could wrap themselves around a tree.

I do not claim to understand their beauties.
Their own sincerities are something they're stupid about.

I am tired of talking technique to the Scottish
who think you have to be parsimonious with a grace before
it will sit on your lap. That's what I have

in common with these boys, the rash taking-for-
granted, their graces strewn behind them,
while the Scottish keep it at arm's length lest they
should be unworthy.
Life is one foolishness or another. Sentimentality is
choosing.

So that I love Italian boys.
I mean the ones here, tempered, distempered by the
unsmiling Wasps, who will always mistake appetite for
blasphemy.

But these boys will always be under a street-lamp
that is supposed to be a Calabrian sun, and they
will become metaphysicians, turning ceilings into
the shingles of heaven and floorboards into
calloused earth —

the Wasps will love this and call it visionary
and the boys will go crazy for this
and hobble back to a street-lamp in a thousand years —
having seen through flattery, the heartless hungers.

And the street-lamp will seem like a thousand suns
and not an electro-sphere for the illumination
of cyborgs;

and they will be at peace with their Catholic mothers
and fathers, since they got their metaphysics from
transubstantiation and their poetry from a happy
Christ, though now they are
unhappy and scared of self-pity.
I would like to wait for them for a thousand years
and hand them the death of the English mind
which they would wave about like cotton candy,
a little sorry, and feeling foolish about the
years they wasted skeptically.

I am so lucky, so ridiculously
lucky; luck oozes from my palm tree,
my fashionable view, sony tv,
lucky in luckiness, lucky in the hands
of the clock, I wheeze luckiness,
lucky in talent, lucky in friends,
lucky in Toronto, lucky to be in Canada, not
Zimbabwe, lucky in health, contacts,
money, I am so lucky — never did an honest
day's work in my life, never wept, never
depressed; I was born chipper, a happy-go-lucky
son of a bitch, never battered, always touched,
spoiled, lucky from the right side of the bed —
and of course absurdly lucky in love —
everything a gift horse. Things are exactly the
way they seem; I was born to the fashion, genes
programmed for sitting in the Courtyard Cafe, all my
books as good as printed as soon as I think of them, poems
coming trippingly off the tongue, my fingers can
barely keep up. What is it to be alone? People appear
magically. What is immigration? What is feminism?
How do you spell rent cheque, suicide, debt. I know
you think I will live forever, so I will. I always
seemed less out at sea than you, because I was born
lucky, to show you up at parties; when you resist me
you will always know there were scores who couldn't.
I will dog you all the days of your life; when you get
close to the top you will always suspect I'll have
gotten there first. You will try to sleep with the
women I have loved. I will publish the story you thought
of writing just as you think you've caught up with
the lucky bugger. What can I do wrong, feeling this
lucky, for you. I can't hate you — it's part of my luck

and even that bothers you. I will always remain a
mystery to you. It sells books, and you will buy them
and understand nothing, and you will feel unlucky.

Ladies and Gentlemen, I present to you a lucky
bastard. If you go to sleep, I will be there when
you wake up, precisely as I was before — lucky.
I of course will have slept less, if at all. I will
have been up writing the poems you wanted to write, loving
the women you wanted, pulling off incredible stunts that
will bring me money, security, romance.

If only I could put my hands around your throat and
squeeze you like a lover. This poem can afford to be
cocky. It will appear blank to you. It is the way
you are — you see what you need to see.
Are you asleep now?
Is anybody there? Please wake up, so I can get
your goat first thing in the morning.
We go back a long way.

Lord, how lucky can anyone be.
You will wake up and you will have missed me.
Another perfect day.
It must be hell for somebody.
Me? I slept fine. I have been around the world
for a long time
and I have landed in your heart, like a vulture,
sad, like a friend, like a lonely hunger
for the hours when you love me.

And friends, do I indeed attract them
because of the type of fellow I am;

yes, I give off good vibes, and the world
returns good vibes to me. I don't attract,
am attracted, cooperated with, and the rays
of sun are pretty intelligent with the
leaves, too.

Nothing is procrastinated. Friends walk in
and out of my room, Glenn, the way you find four of them
in your bedroom after a shoot; they are beautiful
sitting there like that. Mountains sit like that
and clouds.

There is another way of putting this. But I forgot it.
I forget everything. I used to know everything but
I forgot — handy, no? and *vrais.* I forgot what
makes me charming, charismatic and the bones and skin
speak knowledge, and I know more than I think
or care to remember and it shows through. Aware of it
I would be an oaf.
            I love Carol for example the way she
loves skies and bricks outside Jerusalem. Either none
of these things love us, or all of them do and
allow us to love each other.
            It is simply a matter of standing up, ignorant
of what made us happy, sort of like infancy.
            Did you go to a shoot today, did you in fact
photograph the japanese model with scapulas
like flower petals. Or did you appear to do so,
or did you love her by arranging the set? Did the
photograph you took create you, did you create it?

Do you and the model exist outside the photograph,
or in the photograph and outside the photograph as well,
and when you walk into your bedroom back from the
photo session did we not see the photograph?
Who loved the photograph more and did we love you for it?
I did not make you friend, but certainly I stood around
waiting, and there you were happily with arms and legs
and a good "field" around you. It is the unified field
theory. I love you, then. And everything else
eavesdrops, waiting for the precise moment when it can
play at being in us, and with us. The photograph, then,
is also not complete.
There is that matter too.

THE POEM THAT CAN'T HELP ITSELF

I have made this place.
Made out from and away from my own fear,
left far behind for a full day;
that's all it took to become a glory
I had drowned in myself. I resuscitated
the corpse, put a big smile on its face
and said go out and meet people and shake
hands with a ray of light. It was
pathetically simple for me.

And then I met dozens of beautiful friends
who were old enough to be crazy about themselves.
Imagine! People loving and dining
and exercising and, get this, writing books about it —
It's as if they all knew they only lived once. Imagine!
At my age! In this century! In this town!
One of them dumps a seventeen year marriage
and wears a discreet and serious smile.
A couple of them are having an open relationship,
because no one ever gets away from them anyway. It goes on.

So I bought lots of chairs and records and espresso
cups for my friends. And now they all sit around
by turns, the walls being the only hitch, and they
make the place do a kind of astral travel, they make
the area glow. They can never get cancer; all their
energy is transferrable one to another. Whenever
a sadness begins, it gets dissipated by being
passed from one hand to another, so that by the
time it reaches the end of the circle, a tired fear
has gone down among the ranks of the angelic.
It's something like that.
You get the picture.

I cannot even get to sleep, between the excitement of them
thinking about their lives, lives that include each other.
It's like keeping each other up,
like a perpetual morning.

Silly, isn't it. So much euphoria. And there isn't
a thing I can do about it. I am that old. The world
is that old. You can only take it badly so many times.
The man who wants to live is the man in whom life is
abundant. That's all. There isn't a thing to do
about it. A morning like any other, another,
giving itself up, surrendering, with or without the
weather.
And it started when I moved into this new place.
When I opened this that and another thing.
Or maybe my moon was rising.
There's nothing to be done about it. They love me,
and it's at last the perpetual motion machine,
the heart pump that eats food.
If a molecule has it in for us,
there's nothing we can do about it.
        So much for irony.

The throat is dead centre between heart and head.
That is where my language is.
I have no more beauty to tell you about.
I've been forced clean.
How am I supposed to use words like
skive, toy, shout.
I don't believe English words anymore,
body-less things.
I have imaged sounds where the words didn't have any;
put trees in orchards so the wind could be heard
through them; the wind is gone,
back to an old language I have not heard in years,
though I fostered love to approximate it.
What did you think I meant by *the sixties,*
sociology?
Now the words stand still between the heart and head.
Will not come out. *Non vogliano uscire.* Notice how the
word *uscire* is like the word *uccello,* bird; how the
sounds slip into one another to make the mind run
smooth. They don't *make* the mind run smooth, really.
The word *make* is Nordic. That is why there is a war between
heart and head. I never wanted to *make* love.
Ce un velo fra la gola e le parole.
There is a membrane between throat and words.
Where the word should be made flesh.

Furthermore it has always occurred to me that the word
heart should have more than one syllable.

THE AUTHOR DINES WITH FRIENDS IN A
COFFEE SHOP IN LOYALIST TORONTO

These nights are gorgeous.
The gaggle of friends tilting the moon again.
What is there but a minute,
a glass of wine and the derelicts of heart,
heart, the word they have conspired against in this
country.
Bring me a moon, amigos, the amenities of life be
damned, bring me your hand crooked against the cheek,
the tempest of conviviality that dares to sear
the obvious.
I do not want to know too much about my mind.
I have been in and out of its tunnels,
its holograms and models and found a crystal heart
steamed with the breath of desperation, right in the
centre of the folds of the brain, a whining, parched
little heart caught between the bank towers and the
edicts of the just society, a heart like a dog that
wanted to run loose and eat plantain leaves and lap
up the surf. What is this heart doing in Toronto,
I said.
          Amongst my friends the heart was given scraps of
food until it could sit on the table and become
the object of affection.
          The metaphor is banal. This is what happens in
Toronto — what was a sun careening from one memory to
          another
became something that had to be nursed back into health.
The glass of wine my friends is more than blood;
it toasts what can be brought back to life;
we can never get too romantic in this country.
We are too few.
And the kennels are full of the mad.

No more ambition,
please. I had a young man over
tonight and I loved him as I had not loved
him before, and no, dear friends, I am not
talking sex. I am saying how this man
opened up his skull to me and let out
fears and shouts and beauties such as only
curiosity can beat, and this young man had
plenty of that, and I applauded him, no, slapped
him on the back, no, kissed him, as if two angels were
kissing above our heads somewhere above the
January snow; and what a beginning
for the year I mean. The building glowed, the room
glowed and every hero I had ever dreamt of
and this man glowed in his hero-ness, once he saw
it, once we knew how we were brothers,
once we had unpackaged the worst fears
tonight and saw we could be scared of nothing, because
you see, we were curious little angels, and I wanted
to write poems again, because I loved him and suddenly
loved myself, seeing as how he was no different —
anyway I closed the door behind him on the three
thousand miles he would travel back home — and I find
myself saying, "Love. Beautiful, baby, beautiful!" and
sounded like some flower-child and sort
of winced at it and decided some things are more important
and eternally beautiful and style be damned —
and meanwhile I think back on this hack
last week who came over and talked ambition; a
wasted fifty-year-old dead man who sat in front of
me and talked ambition.

Look (and this being the general point of the
         poem) I'm bloody fed up with the
         would be angels we are most of us all
         of the time,
and the rooms can glow, I tell you the rooms can glow, and
how we parcel our fears away from each other and hunt for
love in such abominable half-assed ways, like by ambition —
and just today, and tomorrow morning I want to be a kite,
I want to open up my chest and fly out of myself like a brother
turned hawk.
And I am suddenly grateful for such moments and angry.

If you come to my house bring your ribs and beat me with
them until I confess everything. Don't settle for
less; love me that much. Don't, I say don't discuss
man-woman polarities with me, class problems, books
of how it hurts to be out of circulation. Beat the heart
out of me, and I you until there are only two hearts
on the living room floor. We will pay rent for another
five months for two hearts. They will say, who lives
in apartment 405? I will say two hearts. The world's
skin, a shucked blessing. Something we all boil down to,
hungry for life.

Anyway, the poem is largely out of my system.
But take it as fair notice, in the vicinity of
Bedford and Bloor. It is largely for the vicinity
of my guts and friends and lovers in the
general neighborhood and all vagrants.
I'm not really much interested in the
espresso and tango records, and don't be fooled
by the chi chi lamps and furniture.
Come visit me and be an angel, a planet, a moon,
an incredible set of lungs perched atop a vision;
a pair of legs on wheels that wheel about the planet
and stop off for the benzine of my heart.

DOUBLE BINDS

If you say this stick is real, I'll hit you.
If you say it isn't real, I'll hit you.
If you keep quiet, I'll hit you.
                    — Zen Koan

If you treat me like a woman, I'll hit you.
If you don't recognize me as a woman, I'll hit you.
If you ignore me, I'll hit you.
                    — Feminist Koan

Mother used to do that. "I'm a slave in
this house," she used to scream and boy did she get mad
if I helped myself to the fridge. She wasn't liberated,
I heard, but I love my mother, but she's not
worthy of her self-love, and if I don't see her
I'm an ingrate.   The number *two* was thought
the culprit, the black and white furies. Why not
both man *and* woman. But they'd lie in bed waiting
for someone to make the first move. One or the
other would take the initiative and feel guilty
five minutes into the act for fear of overpowering
the other. The other might want to say no, no, go ahead,
but thought that presumptuous in the liberated
climate, in which birds flitted past the bay windows,
lyrically suggestive of a celerity of bygones.
"Transitional captives" was their assignation.
Their children would have it easier, the way their
grandparents moved easily in their chains,
which were our fabrication we might have thought, but
couldn't go back to subscribing wholesale to. We had to
forge ahead. The word "androgynous" began to sound like
a wished-for hormone, the language eating itself
as we stuffed its mouth with a ball-gag and

held it up for ransom to anyone who wanted to come by
and take it. Our price went lower and lower.
Someone was bound to take it off our hands; and even the
deafening silence would then let up and we'd move to another
part of the country and make a fresh start of things.
These were our real fantasies. Never mind
lulling yourself to sleep with orgiastic visions.
Last things first. There'd be residual libido
waiting around the corner once the pedestals were
scrubbed clean. There wouldn't be erections there,
or penetrations. We dreamed of pure ether, of communions
more kindred to primary programming, Eden
transfusions where the body was just an allegorical
aid for historians. This too was a double bind, next
door to the virgins and the holy water and the original sin
we'd taken on in this state of affairs.
Again, we couldn't get past the number *two,*
and day-dreamed about three hands and asymmetries
that would push us either way past the
polarities and stigmas. To be so much a man that you
didn't need anyone. To be so much a woman
that you didn't need men. It was getting to be
that way, demonstrably when you looked outside,
but cataclysms would occur like vast collective
tidal waves of unspoken fantasies. Our needs
amassed in such a slim body would spill out and
congregate into a natural disaster. A world war,
or an earthquake. Ludicrous! Impossible! we said,
and we'd let Newtonian wonders file our bank notes
rather than own up to our frankensteins.
It was an expiation. We'd project one unhappiness
and let it boomerang back to bite our heads off;
and we'd call it a head of state or an anachronist.
We would admit to nothing, and a love of children was
fostered, dwarfing any historical precedent.
We would rock them in our laps and whisper independence

from the opposite sex. Custody laws would be a thing
of the past, and somewhere men were delivering
babies from the left side of their brains
in laboratories. Like us, they were purists at heart.

We ate in this town
as we usually do, choking
on each other's theories
about living on the edge —
somebody not covering the tip
somebody not making it
with somebody, a career shot
or so it appears — the fantasy of
slipping off to southern climes (I dream
about this regularly)
             tonight I am thinking of
slashing my wrists, outmoded as it is —
slow deaths are original. Preventive
medicine will have to take into account
informational mortar fire over coffee
and repressed neuronal discharges
at a cutting remark; this apartment is like
a ward, I run from one bed to another
nursing various selves, keeping diseases
in check at various levels. Friends phone in
periodically about visiting hours, monitoring
their preferential selves encased in my
body. Doctors should read poetry for the etiology
of death —
             and turn to meteorology for early warning
signs — an existential front moving in from the
north, affecting the social climate. There are days
when everyone is feeling generally bad or good,
and those hybrid urban moods when civilization
makes progress.
             Today I thought of Procrustes, the Greek
innkeeper who lengthened or chopped off the limbs
of his guests to make sure they fit their beds —

and of how the bed I sleep in is not of my making
and every one asks me if I slept well.
      They phone to see if their bed is a better
fit. And the saws are similar —
      yes we are lizard-like and can grow
new tails and the truth shall liberate us
but desperation will make us honest —
and things are never as bad as they seem
and fear is just lack of imagination
      and then there's the man that I took to
the hospital every day and watched fresh
red bags pour new blood into him where he couldn't
make any for himself, and we'd have this
conversation about how his wife had found out
he'd had an affair to avoid getting cancer
but he felt so bad about it he got cancer anyway
and one day, while under morphine, he let it
slip out and how she took care of him anyway,
but threw in the occasional barb
and he used to tell me how she really could
be a little more forgiving — but in the end I heard
him say what I've heard many a man say:
my wife is a saint.
      We know these stories,
so we eat in this town as we usually do —
the food being just an excuse;
anything to keep from dying in the wrong way.
      This poem might be about future orientation
or alienations
or about sharing love and death which is the gift
of those you love,
about loneliness
or about the fact that things do not refer to
themselves, but to other things for completion.
It might be about the formal structures of poems —
the illusion of endings that are the ultimate romance,
only to be able to say *my wife is a saint*

unequivocally, with whatever it takes to be
at rest — to sleep in a bed that fits,
or appears to fit.

      This might be about the monster *human need,*
about saying *I need you* instead of *you are good for me.*
Tonight I will go to a restaurant and meet a good
innkeeper — and it occurs to me why I like
to sleep alone,
why I tuck the covers in at the bottom of the bed
why I sleep against the wall
why my bed has no legs
why lovers snuggle together like spoons
why there are more crimes committed in bed than
in all of legal history,
why the word *art* originally means "to fit,"
why a happy ending has always put me to sleep.

I am a coward, always thinking
of the other guy, never trusting my
words without thought; my insincerities have
banished a thousand lines into a
composite weeping figure, an idiot of
a man I take in and feed periodically
because I disown no one.
But I will get rid of this self-pity one day
and have no patience for others with self-love
and we'll spit sacred days like seeds at the sun,
unparsimonious at last.

I have been a protestant too long. I have had
to confess instead of sing,
and when you confess to other protestants
you get suggestions for editing;

and I pray for the day when I shall not even preach
to feminists out of misguided love —

what have I to do with Utopian gods, I who
knew how to waste time on street-corners
praising the sun by whistling at it — I who

can still remember that, who, for want of
company tried to teach nonchalance.

Like my friend Luciano who wants to play among
Calvinists, I have grown hateful with waiting.
He wears black among them. He is like the angel
of death among the crippled.
What he really wants to do is wear white
at the wedding of the world,
but this is the only job he could get
in a protestant country.

They have given me doubt.
Given is the correct word.

The spirit will be mobile.
Soaring. The myths are dead. They
are trying to kill the myths and me
with them. Side-stepping is in order,
a leap, a somersault with my head
clutched.

It came too easily, they said.
He writes poetry too easily.
This was in a protestant country.
They put strictures on the old girl.

Believing everything, I doubted.
Listening out of love. Listening out of
faith extended. The encompassing self went out.
This was during the sixties.
I did not know a protestant country.

It is too easy, this business of "protestant
country." I hear it already. The carnivorous,
invaginated. Things must be more complex.
The truth must always be more complex.
The wish to suffer is certainly more complex.

That is my only point.
It would not have been a very subtle one
thirty years ago.

I gave her up for what I don't even remember.
She was too fat. Or too awkward. Too loud.
Too Italian. I know that when she walked into a room
she danced it, took the walls apart and filled them
with laughter. I know her voice riveted faith
like a dredged happiness in me.
Maybe I was too Canadian. Maybe the Americans
gave me too many selves to run away with;
maybe I read my happiness like a myth —
I had thought of it too often;
maybe I wished I had died and been buried beside
my father. I do know that she held my hands down
like sunlight on a tired body.
Maybe she had no grace, and I was
like a schoolgirl in her earthen hands.
Maybe we would have had nothing to do
together but devour the continent, and I had
been clever too long. Maybe she hadn't been
killed, and I required a first death.
She brandished my tiredness like a pride,
and she — thirty pounds heavier than me;
maybe I thought death would make her slimmer.
I know she walks into a room now
and she is a vacancy, and now she is light
enough for me and no light at all.
I know that she even lied about carrying
my child in an effort to keep me and for two
years I carried two deaths.
I know there are only dreams walking backwards into
each other, and that I live in a society
where grief is compounded by guilt,
and that her dismissive, jovial hand, virgin

or otherwise took the cankers off accusation.
I know that she was an Italian woman, and I an Italian
man, and that she tried every trick in the book
to keep me, and it was as it should be.
But it was the sixties and I thought about
equality of the sexes. Everything about that
relationship was wrong, as they say.
But when she walked into a room she danced it.
I am in a city of rooms that cannot be legislated
into warmth. Sometimes I think I am
a German idealist. I am no longer involved
in the wrong way at the wrong time.

What the hell am I looking for?
every morning, or afternoon; I wake up
a little confused, reaching out with my arms,
wanting to throw my voice,
desiring a little kiss once in a while.
Maybe even a scratch to give me a sense of
what's real —
maybe a friendship surrounding itself, like a party,
a simple chore of love.

So much for analysis; as far as it ever goes,
as far as the English language, biting its own
tail like the idea of pain, its little chinese
dolls shouting at each other.

With me, it's always been singing;
and the seasons of song, a cicada, the cry of boys
wanting to get out and play, the branch leaning
towards earth at dusk; even the christmas bell,
etching through portals of sound.

Description is analysis, if you have any heart.
As for the conclusions, something should be left to God.
He's what's left over after the weeping,
after the kiss and the wailing —
the repose, evening out as in a mystery,
the oceanic proportions
of faith on a given morning, or on a given night.

The snow falls plentifully; whenever
I have gone out with my friend Salvatore
we have been in a gingerbread landscape —
ostentatiously lyrical, and have
marvelled at it, having been only out together
twice, driving Ontario dirt roads.
We take this as a sign, an unaccountable
augering of the friendship. We move, we realize,
towards a time, when it will be explainable
in terms of the random serialized to
synchronicities of sentimental biospheric fields;
I tell him how even ten years ago people understood
certain things, that even the heart will be a matter
of superstition. Sal and I are driving into the
past, though he thinks he can find his way back,
stop at someone's door and hope to phone home.

The ridiculous will not be tolerated in my later
years. It occurs to me that no one will answer their
door and I won't be cold outside. All my life I have
wanted to withstand great temperatures and life is
making it possible. It is much for a man from the
mediterranean, learning quickly what he would have taken
decades to learn in a vineyard, that the fruits of the
natural are growing under the feet, and can rip you
open like a wisdom come too soon.
I have learned to love winterscapes; they would never believe it
in that other life, that parallel world where I go on
selling tobacco at the Piazza Hotel under the moonlit smiles
of infants in the Prato.
There are many letters that my eyes are.
I can't tell the nineteenth century anything
except what would break its heart.

QUIXOTE TO HIS YOUTH

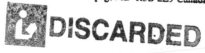
The day will come, I thought, thinking of him,
when you will have to fabricate, daily,
civilization among the bewildered.
Alone, without father and his arias. Like an ideal,
within yourself, populations of twins,
crickets, lunar nights, the caresses of an arm on
your thinking; all things famous in your loving
you will have to imagine like adam in his first step.
You will have to love something other than those you love.
When those you loved are dead or younger.
Pioneer, monument in life, whipped with refrains.
Composer and archivist,
with what swallows will forgetfulness come, sacred,
unmelting; what alms will you have, when
you have given away everything?

II

VIRGIN SCIENCE

" . . . science is thoroughly infused with Puritan ethics; for example, the idea of the scientist, as a predicting and controlling agent for scientific determinism; the 'dogma of immaculate perception' . . . the 'godly discipline' of rigorous experimental minutiae. There is the same rejection of 'speculative questions,' of the private imaginings of subjective personality, of the human image, emotional relationships and reconciling schema in general."

— Charles Hampden-Turner

"Most importantly, the new physics is offering us a scientific basis for religion. This is something new in the history of Western civilization, and its impact will certainly be felt in every aspect of our lives. But a word of caution: the religion offered by the new physics is not a religion of values or absolute principles. It offers no strict delineation of heavens or hells. It is a religion based on the psychology of the human consciousness — indeed, on the psychology of the entire universe as a conscious force acting upon itself. In this new religion we will not find the rules of the game so long sought after by philosophers and theologians. What we will find is a glimpse of ourselves, a bit of cosmic hide-and-seek in which we realize that no rules as such can be found. We make the rules."

— Michael Talbot, *Mysticism and the New Physics*

"In those days my mind was corrupt. I did not know that if it was to share in the truth, it must be illumined by another light, because the mind itself is not the essence of truth."

— St. Augustine

i. THE PROBLEM OF TIME

"Virgins with rulers
and compasses were watching
the heavenly blackboards."
                    — Raphael Alberti

"And Time with us was always popular.
When have we not preferred some going round
To going straight to where we are?"
                    — W. H. Auden

Quantum foam is amniotic.
It is an elegant theory. Elegance involving a
return to the garden. *Worm-holes in space* is
a deathly choice of words. *Womb-holes* might have been
a choicer scientific usage.
But that would have been too transparent, even though
the essence of quantum foam is navigation between
heaven and earth. Black holes, white holes, the haloes of
astral bodies, virtual particles; ecclesiastical
touches on the mechanistic toad.

Mathematics is duel-istic finesse.
Zero is a truce, with evocations of
the divine. Welcome to the world. A sphere with
triangles in it.
There isn't a hope in hell, known as
object differentiation.

PRELAPSARIAN: The Mother of Time

"Fables that time invents to explain its passing . . ."
— John Ashbery

Time. She is coming.
Mother. There was no time before her.

She brought it with her
feeding time.
If *she* was late, we grew up unfulfilled.
If *she* was timely, we wound up unfragmented,
with a sense of timing.
Now she talks about the best years of her life
and the ten good years before the war.
I grew up nostalgic for her past.
I grieve twice over,
for the fall from her womb
and for her fall from grace.
She must have done something terrible
to have had only ten good years; as if the angel
came down and deemed her unfit.
I have to live her down.
I am the virgin maker
The sanctifying angel,
the penitential prodigal for her.
The second coming.

She is coming. She will feed my body.
She teaches hunger and heaven.
She builds the house of time.
I will build my own and dwindle to
a point of singularity.
But I must make her virgin first,
travel backwards in time, catch her
before her grief and follow her and be

her grief, to understand the sin
that is nostalgia.
Then I will sanction her. And say:
Corrupt, you are beautiful, and your son will be
down to earth and never leave you. He is coming,
and he is redeemed.

●

My brother died during the war, before I
was born. His name was Giorgio. His death
was original. I am his sin.
That is one story.
I am the maker of another.

Virgin fictions. There is no end to them
And no beginning. The light is virginal
this morning. She is everywhere I make her
out to be.

The virgin
making.

THE ORPHEUS OF TIME

"I must not allow my mind to insist that time is something objective."
— St. Augustine

Measuring one thing against another
is how you build the time memorial.
Time irreversibility is a consequence of
the measurement process.
Old people lose memory
so they can live in the past.
They appear bored. There is a tense in
which their minds are on a long vacating.

●

History remembers.
History propels us
by hope
or object differentiation.
Object lesson: the amniotic and the air.
The body was hopeless.
It did not starve for an idea, until later.

●

Memory is what you get when you can't eat
when you want.
In the womb, you're always eating.
Out of the womb, there is being fed and not
being fed . . . the food of love, and no food of
love, and music, to remind you
of how good you had it.

●

He tried to drown himself. His
life flashed before his eyes.
Time reversibility. The thought of not being
fed, ever again, saved him from himself.
But remembering someone saved him. Thanks for the memories,
the time savers.

●

When I was seven years old I lay on a bed
with my mother and a clock. For three days
she taught me to tell time, feeding time,
hard times, the best of times, minute hands trying
to catch up with hour hands, and missing. I miss
those days. She put time before us.
Father time. Killing time.
The scythe. Umbilicus.
There was an obvious connection.

●

During sensory deprivation or sensory overload
duration shortens. Time feels amniotic.
On a beach, in Greece, you feed.
Stars, wind, water. Timelessness.
You forget.
You make love
to forget.
You unmeasure the body from hope
to forget.
You forget nothing, to glut memory.
You forget everything, to starve memory.
You try everything once.
You are fascinated by amnesiacs.
No death is untimely enough.
You worship circles

and myths that help you remember why
you want to forget.

•

Heart is the artefact of memory.
The art of forgetting facts.
If you are an artist they will feed you for this.

•

Amniotic   Amnemonic

Words from the time marmorial

Scientific curiosity is a redressing of object loss.

Between fifteen and twenty-four months the child begins
to bring objects back to mother to "show her." She verifies
their existence. Empiricism does the same job.
Mother gives out Nobel Prizes, Greenwich Mean Time,
and the speed of light constant.
The measurement process sees to it that time is
irreversible. Mother sees to it that you can
never go back. The mother, it follows, is
seen as a witch.
Feminism therefore should concern itself with the
excision of Newtonian programming in the pregnant
woman's head. It is a man's world by
default from the garden.

GRAVITY AS FALL: The Cosmogonization of Object Loss

Newton was born on Christmas Day, 1642. Prematurely.
His father died three months before he was born. Newton
suspected a virgin birth. When his mother abandoned him
at three years of age to go and live with another man, he
remained in the care of his grandmother and then went out
to cement his object loss, conjuring all of Europe into
believing his phantasmagoria of gravity. All bodies
attracted to one another. Prima mater, matter dolorosa.
Matter that can never go home.

Newton haunts nurseries. Before Newton, infants were
reported not to have fallen out of bed. Parents are
Newtonian fabulists. All stories about changelings are about
Messianic delusion.
Newton's ghost shudders with delight.
It was Newton who first wanted to be more
popular than Christ.

There's no question that gravity is real.
Newton and Descartes saw to that
and Galileo dropped self and non-self from the tower
and observed that they plummeted at equal speeds.
Father, son and holy ghost.
Self, non-self, and gravity. They didn't see the connection.

Falling, falling from your mother.
Motion is a heart-breaker.
Gravity is the home-coming.
The return of the holistic ghost,
to confirm the virgin birth.

Newton's mother hit him on the head.
He remembered something about Eve
munching in Heaven.

RELAPSARIANS: Lovers in Newtonian Time

The photon entering your eye was emitted by a star
in the past. It was too late for the wise men;
they arrived to find the manger tainted
with event.
It is always too late.
We are always trying to catch up.
We reassemble the manger and re-enact
how lovely it must have been.
We are omitted from the present.
Cumulative omissions enlarge the myth
of you and me, with so many tardy
romances behind us. I expect you to raise
your hand to my cheek the way I imagined it.
It is only later that it will seem perfect.
I will talk about you to another, and she will
reassemble what might have been between us.
They call this listening to the needs
of the other. These are all historic relationships.

Who you are will dawn on me later.

A LA BELLE ÉTOILE: Wishing in Bi-lateral Time

Always later. Tardy messengers with passion
in envelopes, to be opened later. Do not open
until, the stars fall down, contrite, recursive,
towing us up so that we can lead someone astray for
a change.
It was love at first sight, the instant I saw you.
Sure thing. Like the changeling in the
manger, in place of longing, which tires us by now.
There is no sureness,
Schrödinger's cat is alive or dead
depending on perception.
Open me first, me, not him; the right order, then
everything will fall into place, eacah star whimpering
like a pup, cradled by a child, the genetically
hushed need to materialize the coming.

It is always the second coming. The seconds coming
at me with news of your thought a while ago.
Now. I want it now. The baby screams, unused to
time withheld. Perhaps he was a moonbeam in another life,
sailing through the rooms of cosmos,
willing before and after like leapfrog, hurdling what
would become his longing.

STRATAGEMS FOR THE ULTRA-TEMPORAL

"Three coins in the fountain. Each one bringing happiness."

The number *three* is noteworthy. It is a holographically significant number and trinity-like. The movie from which the song is taken was filmed in Rome, not two miles from the Vatican. This mixing of religion with happiness is notoriously Italian. That each coin should bring happiness is statistically unlikely; besides, it leaves the future to chance, which doesn't improve the odds in a universe in which micro-particles have a fifty-fifty chance in any quantum event. This is not a pessimistic gloss; though I admit to the bitterness of a man weaned on traditions in which the random has been assigned religious-romantic valences of probability. Hope was the deterministic lever by which dream could faithfully be accomplished with the warranty of laboratory results. Albeit the beakers were hearts, the compounds sensorial, and the data anniversary-like. The fountain had the characteristic of looking like mutability bounded. This was reassuring. If time was a river, it had been captured. The coins looked translucent in the water as if the temporal had been chucked into the timeless. In fact, matter and time alter each other and twist in a dreamy, usually indiscernible manner, though Einstein's theories yielding the space-time continuum could not have had a conscious impact on the three girls who tossed the coins in the fountain with the abandon of girlish impulsiveness. As usual, empirically-tested results have a way of entering the poetic consciousness ahead of anyone's time. The director is to be credited for playing a good hunch and writing the coins into the script. He too was unwitting and should have taught me Newtonian grade-ten physics instead of the oaf in a suit and tie who never went to the movies.

    The girls are standing beside their fiancées as they toss the coins in. This is really like thumbing your nose at chance. I remember learning not to count my chickens before they hatched, and failing physics and taking remedial lessons under Jerry Vale and Frank Sinatra.

"The mechanical constructs of
Space-time are by definition
Not accessible to the will.
That is why they were invented."
— Kenneth Rexroth

Photons travel at the speed of light from the moment they are created, without ever having been accelerated from a slower speed. Always were, are, and always shall be. We, on the other hand, would grow indefinitely large as we approach the speed of light. That's why the speed of light is a constant. It assumes the body is a temporally bounded entity. This is medieval and ignores the marked retreat of measurable body frequencies during altered states and the popular fact that you can sneak up on somebody by riding in the blind spots of a person's consciousness. Speed of light constants ignore the crass disappearance of matter dolorosa or the surprise at change before we investigate it. Such is the artificial instilment of wonder in the world, just to downplay the random. This offers a religious double bind. God is perfect but as we can never achieve the speed of light without stretching on the cosmic wrack, we can scourge ourselves with the moral implications of the atom bomb. It is neurotic and convenient. What appeared unassuming in Einstein was conscience-stricken. His curiosity did double time on Jungian freeways of photon travel and woke up in the morning to fall from the garden. He was a model romantic.

Alice keeps looking through the keyhole, mooning about a point of singularity, wishing God would cut her down to size. She is a great feminist Cartesian heroine. Her lust compresses her and she weeps a diffuse medium that will carry her through the keyhole. In essence, she is spreading herself thin to bypass Einstein's injunctions against bounded bodies. Her despair makes her talented. It is the ultimate Catholic fantasy.

The keyhole is a wormhole, black hole, space/time warp, doorway to another dimension, glimpse of the infinite, etc. It makes no difference to the body of language.

Presumably, after her saga, Alice sports a halo of photons, as an afterwash of her speed of light experiences. She remains a virgin since her victories over classical physics are unwitting. This makes her especially sexy to mathematicians. It makes them feel that divinity does not come easy.

It ensures the unmade virgin in themselves.

It is a constant.

LUX AETERNA

" . . . l'amor che move il sole e l'altre stelle."
—Dante

"The further away a distant galaxy is, the faster its velocity of recession; there comes a point at which a galaxy is so far away that its recessional velocity equals the speed of light."
—Michael Shallis

Gravity and evolution were lovers. They invented moms
and dads who didn't want their children to stray from
them in crowds. The kids have inertia. Other things
are always tugging at them, cotton candy, strangers,
puppy love. There is orbital laughter and spheres of
influence that weep. Kids give in because they're light-
headed. Now it's an idea, now it's sex, a blue sky.
Gravity.
Everyone wants to keep you, everyone wants to keep still
and grow in mass, to carry a lot of weight — your heart,
your bones, anything will do. Evolution wants us to
gain weight.

●

Don't leave me, don't ever leave me.

●

Some conscious phenomena travel at the speed of light:
e.g. I'm still here, but I've already left this relationship.
e.g. the idea of the cotton candy, before dad lets go of
your hand. Any dream.
Evolution hates this. Gravity goes to the dungeon.
Babies can't be made at the speed of light.
Civilization. The nice policeman. Returns you.

58

●

The body dies. At the speed of light there is no
death. Evolution needs your body. The farthest galaxy
is singing, home, in no language. Language is the
bogy of gravity in your skull.

●

Don't leave me; don't ever leave me!

●

Meanwhile, you love light.
You can't get enough of it.
It gets dark too soon.
Evolution says, go to bed.
Gravity says, don't get up yet,
your feet are tired.
Sleep. Everyone is asleep.
The kiss that wakes everyone is so simple.
Love happens at the speed of light.
You dream this, you hear the singing
in your sleep.

●

Leave or don't leave. You are the sempiternal.

ii. THE ESCAPE FROM MATTER

"We pay a large price for a material world. The price involves our sanity. We cannot make total order of our observations. There always appears to be something missing. This disruption of God's order appears to us as the Principle of Uncertainty."

— Fred Alan Wolf,
Taking the Quantum Leap

"When our descendants seek to define our times, they will probably make use of the term 'neo-Manichaeanism' to describe our characteristic resentment of evil Matter to which we desperately oppose value, but value no longer flowing from a divine source and now exclusively human, like a Baron Munchausen able to pull himself from the swamp by his own hair."

— Czeslaw Milosz

THE PRE-RAPHAELITE UNCERTAINTY PRINCIPLE

"The knowledge of a position of a particle is complementary to the knowledge of its velocity or momentum. If we know the one with high accuracy we cannot know the other with high accuracy."
— Werner Heisenberg

One thing at the expense of another, looking at, I overlook
this other thing about you, absorbed was I in preternatural
looks, your promiscuity escaped unseen; fuelled was your
iris by letters of birch when you were sixteen, such beauty
distracts. Knowledge means ignorant; it takes you someplace,
vantage-rich, your back turned to
murderous elseness, tomorrow's child. Knowledge impasse.
Epistemological binds.
Handcuffed to an axiom I strafed down the garden
moonlight looking at, why not, couldn't dive into
blue-bells, vortices with the gravity of longing.
My need that great why do the laws not bend
in my classical torso in a cosmos that kisses me not.

SYMMETRIES OF EXCLUSION: Duo-Genesis

"Teach us to care and not to care"

       — T. S. Eliot

Heisenberg's uncertainty principle has been a thorn in my heart for years. It is a physical justification for all symmetries of exclusion. I can still hear my mother saying I can't have everything — that I have to choose. Subtler phoenicians of the real world said I couldn't be in two places at once, that I couldn't have a modern woman and a traditional woman. Things seem to slip from between your fingers unless you pay no attention to what you're doing. Art is the science of duplicating accidents. That is why artists exhaust themselves at cause and effect, drugging their bodies or burning themselves out. What is left over is nonchalance. It's what you fool matter with to make it act natural.

  Heisenberg was a twit. His marital situation should have alerted him to the either/or behaviour of particles. The obvious escaped him, not unlike the knowledge of either position or momentum.

  The choice of the world "complementary" is poignant. The word palliates the dogged acceptance of polarities. It's as if his love-making had crept into his scientific-linguistic underwear. That's mean. But why be patient with Calvinists? Let them get to heaven on their own time, without sacrificing the superluminal potential of the race.

It's like seeing flecks on your eye and trying
to focus on them. They skitter off.
You look the other way and they hold still
for you in your peripheral vision. A rough act
of observation embraces nothing.

You can't have it both ways. This groins me.
Ignorance isn't just bliss, it's a methodology
worth praying for from the standpoint of knowing
a little too much and not enough,
like sitting in palm trees and watching
the chevrolet become the impala by watching
your girlfriend neck with your best friend.
It's delirious, screwing your head around by
making sense, and getting silly and being taken
seriously in a room at the party you had no notion of.
Oh well, at least you have a shop you can call your own;
it doesn't matter if the wholesalers are a little
late. You can sit on the straw chair beside the
fruit stands and smoke wisps of afternoon light.
If someone comes in and buys a cabbage you can write it
off as your winning nonchalance.
The wife is patient and she understands the variables
that make survivalist art. You think of returning
to school for those courses you always wanted to take,
but it seems an act of supreme disturbance now that
you've mastered the quotidian frustration into the
honest dollar. It's an apex of sorts, attenuated to
fill holidays and early awakenings and moments of
grand joie under the evergreen. Every once in a while
you remember something about the first black and white
bouts, but you were younger and you wouldn't wish it
on your children. You cast the thought out, inextricable

as it is with your younger self, whom you might almost
miss, like the glimpse of your moustache as you answer the door
running from the bedroom to the hall. The mirror in between
affords a moment you're bound to get back to. Plenty
of time for that, in the order of things, out of this world.

SEARCHING THE LIGHT CONE: Mind over Matter

"The World of the quantum-solipsist bears some resemblance to Descartes' 'I think therefore I am.' A quantum-solipsist says: I am the only reality. Everything out there is in my mind. To change reality — that is, to change objects into different objects — I need to change my mind."

— Fred Alan Wolf

Matter appears solid because electrons
rotate at 600 miles per second.

That's pretty slow. The body is also a dullard.
Try to get your hands in
past the propeller.

The institutional is a speed trap.

No thing has broken the thought barrier.
186,281 miles per second.

Most attempts at teleportation of objects
end in degrees of self-levitation.
The causally-minded are shattered.

Dead weight is the reality structurer.

Squeeze in.
Take everything with you.

Reality is the sandbag in a balloon gondola.
Drop what you're doing.
That's from a longitudinal point of view.

Omnidirectionality is your best bet
with the electron.
Act naturally. The path of least resistance.
Fake a pass. Think Newtonian and
dash the other way.

Matter gets used to being an impasse.
The homeostatic use of your limitations.
You drape continuity over the
furniture and stay home.

When the sun comes up next morning
it is cheerful. It is the only thing
you've seen for days that goes through
windows.
It's prodigal.

THE IMMATERIALIST: The Magic of Mind over Matter

"The greatest wizard would be the one who bewitched himself to the point of accepting his own phantasmagorias as autonomous apparitions."
— Novalis

Lovers. The funeral pyre of dualism.

Idealization as the multi-dimensional
hologram incarnate.

He fell off the cross and splintered into locality.
An arm here, a leg there. Uproarious cumulous laughter.
Generations of specialists.

Believing is seeing. Not a ghost of a chance with her.

The auto-seductive universe in an act of faith.

•

External reality is the big conjuration,
the professional irony.
The illusion matters, so you throw the wand away.
Literature is
the magician having second thoughts about
having thrown the wand away.

The wand can be internalized
for safe-keeping. This was done extensively
during the age of reason, something like drawing
the head into the shell, lovers retiring together
behind closed doors, away from the climate of
legislation.

When magicians decide to stop conjuring and
clear up the backlog, physicalism results.

Science after Newton starts to look like the journey of the
magi with Newton as Messiah.

The situation is in tenses.
Help me forget what I already know in
the superluminal sense, the past present
and future in the palm of my hand.
Redeify me, since we initially chopped ourselves
up to have someone to play hide-and-seek with,
magicians who have believed their own apparitions.
This was done with skilled ignorance. Self-invoked
to logic we smell omniscience like supper odours
from around the corner. The others are shouting
This is the real world, you're crazy.
The air is thin and logical.
You are subject to idyllic dreams.
You start talking in terms of a fall from the garden.
This is acceptable.
If you can persuade them that position and velocity
are not divisible they'll call the game off.
The dawn of creation has passed, the sun under
those red brick houses.
You can either give the benefit of the doubt
or start talking to stones and galaxies.
You have sex periodically to check out the
superluminal potential of the organism.
This is a matter of conscience as much as anything else.
Soon it will be important to benefit from all the
doubts.
There is nothing boring about it.
You celebrate Christmas, one child, one manger.
You keep your mouth shut. You pretend that light
takes years to travel, that you haven't been here before.
You make wishes, tautologically, to make
things come true. The room is full of
sleepy conjurers, roughly the size of

children. In dreams they put on their vast
robes again and weep mournfully.
For a long time now, I have had
insomnia.

incorporated their wands,
after the fashion of their day
and went into the professions.

Metaphysics was their field colony for years
although they eked out existences like defunct explorers
stealing from the fleet at night.

A certain loneliness, orphaned
from civic use, a biding.
Playing down the alchemical,
posturing as artists for safety.

Until they became just lovers, mindless
of the ancient trade,
idiot savants, irked in their sleep
by collective dreams, ritual crowd noises
from benign enclaves.

Everybody loves a lover. Bequests like bread.
Their bestowals memorialized in a locket, a tale
for grandchildren.

Lover avoiding lover, picking only
the heedless, the sacrilege, repelled
by their own kind for fear of harming
with half-knowledge.

These are not saints,
nor historical. They are the recollections
of those not made much of at the time.
Their aggrandizements are the quality of air,
a somatic change like a heart leaping.

The wands of their bodies, sheathed
in the common day resonate so that you
might care to walk by them. A light touch.
An illumined fossil
of the extinct.
An availability.

THE WARLOCK OF THE SELF-REFERENCE COSMOLOGY
SPEAKS

"Things are real only after one has learned to agree on their realness."
— Carlos Castaneda

Matter as the abrupt interaction of fields.
Maintained three dimensionally by the need for
continuity.
Infants half-believe matter. They do or don't get burned.
Tears are the criterion. The appearance of burns is
an optical illusion. If enough people believe in
the same optical illusion, the infant will die.
He must appear to have died.
               Bodies are existential try-outs.
               If new-born bodies won't fit the
belief ecology of a world, the kid retreats to
a star like Sirius B, habitable, in an
unobservable time-frame.
               This is Sirius B where infants are free from not
very original sins.
               The tenacity of infants that choose to live
can be explained by genetic bleachers filled with
ancestral fans, all of whom loved mind-body splits.
               Infant mortality was pervasive before
the advent of bicameral mind.

P.S. The particular parish
where Isaac Newton was born
had an exceptionally high
rate of infant mortality.

Matter, you optical illusion, you,
all because I bite visuals off in large
chunks, because I am not small and can't
get through the keyhole to where hadrons
are departing for every place I ever loved.
It saddens me. Really. To see you taken so
seriously, verbatim, enlarged with every
credulous bastard.
Nowhere like the present; in time there will be
nothing like that. And I for one will mourn nothing
but my smallness. Cut you down to size in the alba.
If there were one thing like the next I'd
tell the bankers, and get loaded down with
manna. Not in this world. I hear the drifting
notes from the universe next door. They're using
our shadows for soccerballs and we left something
in them like grief.

Matter; nothing more than the transform and
organization of field quanta. Quanta-fied.
The overlap of haloes, as if the concentric
haloes of the madonna had boomeranged out
and looped you and zeroed back with your
aura hooped to her own. Now that's idealism,
miles between the causal. The
material, mater, umbilical to itself.
Wombholes into dimensions, into the fabric of
space-time, by dunking your head into epiphany
and coming out the other side of pathos, not
getting the whole body through. Cheap divinations,
this side the grave.

THE REDEEMING OF MATTER

"Matter is nothing but gravitationally trapped light."
                                    — Jack Sarfatti

1. I have a renewed respect for the gravity of any situation.

2. Materialists would do well to read Petrarch.

3. Tachyons are particles that move faster than light.
   Inspiration is made up of tachyons. That is why when
   you're inspired the room disappears around you.
   This also works if you are trapped in an elevator.

4. This is why time disappears when you're writing a poem.
   Time stops at the speed of light. When you think that fast
   you can do time travel. A sense of eternity,
   a sense of history.

5. Nothing matters when you untrap light. Tachyons.
   Out of body experiences are tachyon travel. When you're
   bored you can think of being somewhere else.
   I wish I were somewhere else, is lack of imagination.
   Take the body with you.

6. Imagination is love. Love is inspiration.
   Everyone wants the speed of light. To get out
   of the body. That's why sex. Sex without love is
   fast running.

7. I want to be loved by you
   Just you
   And nobody else but you —
       This is sung by people who are tired of speed of light
       travel. They want to settle down.
       Or they get dizzy.

8. At the speed of light, you don't make money.
   When you step off the time machine, they want
   the rent cheque,
   in any century.

9. Why is it we don't always travel at the speed of light?
   In order to make babies. Evolution wants us to stick around
   for at least nine months. This takes time.
   This is where women want you to act down to earth.

10. Dreamers are often travelling at the speed of light.
    That's why they don't seem to be here. They're always
    somewhere else.

11. Matter and light are an old dualism. The virgin mary
    was illumined by a bright angel. This is the best of
    all parallel worlds. It's holism.

12. Why *gravity* in the first place?
    A fulcrum between heaven and earth.
    See-sawing is not believing.
    Just to have grave consciousness,
    birth consciousness.

13. Nothing matters after all.
    That's a long time on the see-saw.

14. A year ago, I bought a black leather jacket.
    So people could see me.
    It worked. It made anti-matter, in so far as
    they thought me a rebel to materialism.
    This way I can have speed-of-light thoughts and
    it's okay, since they think I'm
    basically against the Establishment —
    Actually I'm anti-matter. A neat poet's trick.
    They let me into classrooms.

15. My argument is against gravity.
    My vengeance for falling out of mother's womb.
    I was. I didn't need this world.
    Just to fly just to fly.

16. The gravity of language. I am the fulcrum.
    It is the cross. To get the language at the speed
    of light. The holistic ghost.
    To abscond to heaven, body and all.

17. Or as my friend's six year old son
    said last Easter. You know, at the end of the
    world, it will be the Easter bunny.

iii. THE GALLERY OF HOLISTIC SCIENCE

"This world view of modern physics is a systems view, and it is consistent with the systems approaches that are now emerging in other fields, although the phenomena studied by these disciplines are generally of a different nature and require different concepts. In transcending the metaphor of the world as a machine, we also have to abandon the idea of physics as the basis of all science. According to the bootstrap or systems view of the world, different but mutually consistent concepts may be used to describe different aspects and levels of reality, without the need to reduce the phenomena of any level to those of another."

— Fritjof Capra, *The Turning Point*

A HOLOGRAPHIC THEORY OF CONSCIOUSNESS:
The M.I.T.-Descartes Scrimmage

Material objects are the result of two or more intersecting sets of waves married into three dimensional forms by the act of consciousness. Consciousness as the pure light of the laser beam. Half of the beam goes directly to the photographic-holographic plate (memory) while the other half is reflected onto a fresh percept, picks up that information and travels on to the memory plate.

Percepts are always changing.
The beam is always on.
The memory plate swells with information,
      is at the mercy of the strength of consciousness
which is divided (the bicameral mind).
That is: on the opposing side of the memory plate (so to speak, since the three dimensional is metaphoric) is the eye of self-consciousness, peering through the memory plate at an oblique angle so as not to be caught in the direct light of consciousness.
The eye is the ventriloquism of consciousness.
The light beam of consciousness and the eye are connected by
faster-than-light signals called *free will.*
On a neurological level they communicate in a synaptic vessicle 400 A in diameter and can only be heard to decide among themselves (the analogue is an act of awareness) in an area of 50 A. The room they talk in is almost spherical, and they whisper. In order to be described (they love being talked about) they get us to use the neuro-physiological mechanism as a Rosetta stone. Though any paradigm would do.

To indulge them (consciousness and self) let's say that the laser-light of consciousness occurs in the pineal body, midpoint in the brain. It occurs there but originates in the interaction of energy fields throughout the brain, the body and the surrounding ecosystem. The brain is just an amplifier. The self looks through the memory plate, and makes

meaning of the interference patterns.
It's so good to see you.

•

A felt hologram is an interference pattern set up by the memory of
emotional relationships. In this case, relationships (romantic or
familial) can be seen as intersecting sets of waves. When the waves are
"in phase" (their crests moving in unison) it occurs to me that I love
you. Dozens of "father" waves, "mother" waves and the waves intrin-
sic to that afternoon we had at Indian Head Resort in the White
Mountains of New Hampshire. When relationship waves are out of
phase (their crests clashing against each other) it occurs to me that I
should dump you. i.e. my father touched me and you don't.

•

In another dimension the self-conscious "I" becomes self-important
and starts taking the neuro-physiological paradigm seriously. It starts
dropping faster-than-light signals like a bad juggler. Consciousness
retaliates by illuminating only a small portion of the memory plate.
This still permits the eye to see the memory hologram, but in less
sharply defined detail and from a decreased range of possible points of
view. The resultant state of mind is called pigheadedness and requires
a bifocal lens like language to reconstruct fifty-fifty vision.

   This is ironic since 50 A might be the order of magnitude of the
latitude in which consciousness operates in interaction with the
neuro-physiological mechanisms of the brain, within the limit allowed
by Heisenberg's Uncertainty Principle.

   This is commonly known as a mind-body split.

All possible histories of the universe occur and
interfere with each other,
intersecting. Events are holograms in time, riding
volitional quanta fed by the self-conscious
or the unconscious. Everything interferes with everything
else. The universe is subset after subset of holograms.
Each subset is a metaphor for the "larger" hologram. Those
who entertain the larger hologram become hysterical.
The laughter of epic-phenomenon. The God-in-hiding pokes
his head up. He is worse than the medusa. He turns your
body to light, so no one can see you.
There are micro-holograms and
macro-holograms, and the mind is skiving the apple.

   The apple was sliced to ribbons before it ever fell.
   The hunger continues.
   Becomes a hunger for ideas. The God-in-hiding
grins.

Marriage is an institutional hologram.
In the eyes of the witness.
The two caught in the act,
reactivated by the record, caught on film,
the memory plate, republicized by language.

Reillumination of plates, anytime
on the lazy susan, by rings, the frozen ripples
of the pond they sat beside a-courtin'.
The word *wife,* reactivates the hologram at the
disposal of, refers to the
reference beam in everyone's pocket, like a handgun,

the undulations of two lovers, caught in
the act, the public eye; it is the discontinuation
of ripples in a pond for the record.

The priest is more than a technician.
He is what the white light wears,
the virgin light more virginal than
the bride. She is an image, sacrificial
to the memory bank.

They are married to,
they do not marry.
They are married to re-cognition, being seen
again in a different light. Being seen.
The whole point is visibility. The witnesses.
The hunger of the all-seeing eye,
ritually mobile.

They get tired of locking the door to their room.
They get tired of locking the door to their room.

At birth the brain has roughly as many neurons
as there are stars in the galaxy. There is a
chance of meeting creation halfway. Entropy
jumbles the puzzle by schismogenesis. A cortical
numbers racket with an understanding of the
number 100 billion. Pick up stochastic errors
with time slipping between fingers. Or pull the
symmetries in like shutters overlooking the
momentary flowers. There is another concept failing
you like the weather. Behind you someone says "it is
raining." Now you have raindrops and the reference
to raindrops. You adore silences, or greater
redundancy, which are the same. To sleep in the
propagations of fractions. To trip backwards over
the replications of God. You have married a
boring man. It is a masterpiece. A mid-life teeter,
with both of you demented with the random side
of the climb.

The dwarf star Sirius B, as it becomes a black hole is slipping behind earthly time more than a second every five hours.

Watching the world go by. The mass of memory-laden consciousness slows time down, so that old people watch the world going faster around them. Their physical deceleration is a blind spot to us as a black hole appears a vacancy in interstellar space. Death is the point of singularity, a foetal approach to timelessness and a fulcrum similar to the white hole/black hole nexus.

Inversely proportional, desire and attainment in dreams are symbolized by the loved one running to catch up with another loved one. The faster one goes, the faster the other recedes. These are races against time; causal embarrassments.

Unfocussing distends the quantum matrix of the body, breathing light, slowing time down just enough to be in touch with the past. Greater diffusion of consciousness will plummet you too far back or too far forward at the speed of light. What you want is a good feeling of continuity. Of being at home in the world. History intact.

Of course when loved ones die, you want to leap to their retrieval. You fish for them in the quantum foam. While mourning, you are lost to others. The body, unaccustomed to speed-of-light travel, falls back into the room, pulling your consciousness in after it like a guy-rope.

You remember these trysts fondly, and wonder at your element. After many such excursions, reunion with the dead does not seem so traumatic.

You can't kill anything before it multiplies.
Every quantum transition is splitting the world up
into myriad copies of itself.
So much for the question of free will.
And don't ask me if I'm political.
I've never known a moment that wasn't
a tearful junction of hellos and goodbyes.

Intense people generate vast numbers of
quantum transitions.
This can be dangerous or exciting depending
on your insistence on carrying on.
When you meet her, she'll turn your head
around.

Or be civil. Each person is allowed
an awareness of their quantum potential
commensurate with their education. The state
monitors ensure that group telekinesis will
not be a threat. If banknotes are to disappear
it will be accidental. The weather will decide.

Dream on. Collective out of body experiences
burgle The Secretary of Statistical Quantum.
I'll see you in my dreams.
When Jung was a child he readily admitted to
anything he was accused of. Not because he
had done anything, but because he knew that
in some universe of possibility he might

have done it.
We are imaginative, until proven innocent.

History is written by copy-cats.
Existentialism is really a problem of
which parallel universe to swear into.

PAN-PSYCHIC NOCTURNE

"For I thought of spiritual things, too, as material bodies, each in its allotted place."   — St. Augustine

THE UNIVERSE IS NOT contiguous in space or
time. Quorums of naming establish their own
ideatic fields behaving like electromagnetic
fields. Believing is seeing. The collective
monocle descends in the night sky like a filter.
The socio-ideatic field stretches as far as the
lake, unrelayed across water because of the
sheer absence of believers. Precious memories
transmute into the moist *deva* of moss, lichen,
sunken ships. Beyond the lake there
is an island where you are not prone to suggestion.
      Buildings on the mainland, morphically maintained
by the gravitational synergies of group intention.
It takes a whole city to keep a building up.
Every once in a while sub-urban desire shifts like
loose earth, and a building collapses. The city, like
a topographical handprint realigned in cosmopolitan
dreams. There is a forest where the tree is not a tree
but which the forest feels to itself like a hand.
The tree falls because the hand is tired. In the
city there is a hand that branches into the
soft hair of a woman. Form changes in the ideatic
field. It takes three, four, a hundred people to
make you change your mind. They keep your head together,
your brains from spilling into communion.

Mini-black holes infiltrated the universe after the big bang. If they are microscopic they can disturb the ecology of relationships, elbowing their way into discussions and formulations of thought. They gorge themselves on time. A black hole the size of a micro-particle can affect one of two people having a conversation. The black hole manifests itself as an instant of inattentiveness while it moseys its way through the brain, warping neurological pathways in much the same way as a bow bends a violin string, modulating time. This accounts for some time lags between thought and speech. Clusters of black holes loiter indefinitely in matter, giving rise to the sentimental value of heirlooms. They are nourished by the absorption of the light of consciousness drawn from the pineal node. The observer contemplating such objects of sentimental value will feel "as though time had stopped." He will, in fact, be experiencing the event horizon of the black hole. Mini-black holes can have a slingshot effect on thoughts, already accelerated by inspiration, propelling the host into heightened states of consciousness. Some black holes behave parasitically, lodging in a person's bio-gravitational field for years. They cannot be removed. They will drop off of the electromagnetic exoskeleton of the host like beads of water after a shower. After love-making especially, when the body is saturated with faster-than-light particle interactions, the black hole starves and falls. The host is then seen to have blossomed, or to have "come into his own," to "have had an *awakening*," etc.

The other side of a mini-black hole is a mini-white hole. Together they form a teacup handle on three dimensional space. This handle is hollow and provides a superluminal shortcut between vast distances. One person's thought fragment can tag on to another person's thinking, city to city. An artful subconscious can predict the position and inertial effect of black holes and time itself for a propulsion into far-away places. It is a means of keeping in touch with loved ones, or overloading the event synergies of the Secretary of State.

TOWARDS A TRANSFORMS GLOSSARY: The Depolarization of Plato's Cave

"I suspected that this transition from one form to another might take place by means of an intermediate stage in which they were deprived of all form but were not altogether deprived of existence."
— St. Augustine

A metaphor is an abstract topological conversion.

Topology was heretofore a branch of geometry concerned with the way in which figures are connected, rather than with their shape or size. Topology is concerned with the geometrical factors that remain unchanged when an object undergoes a continuous deformation (e.g. by bending, stretching, or twisting) without tearing or breaking.

Intuition is a topological conversion of such rapidity that it is taken to be qualitatively different than logic.

Topological conversions may occur at the speed of light.

A transform is a coded version of old information. The smallest unit of information is a difference that makes a difference. Information propagates information; a process of continuous fusion. The word "fusion" here signals that a topological conversion has taken place on a semantic level and on the level of metaphor. No information has been lost. The universe conserves information.

Written metaphors are transforms in suspended animation. The metaphoric shift of this sentence is too quick to be

true. Therefore: written metaphors are like microchips;
information that is dormant until activated by memory circuits.

Paradigms are a matter of taste.

Synaesthesia is a sensorial topological conversion.
No information is lost.
A man blind from birth sees with his ears.
The word "sees" here replaces complex mathematical
transforms describing bio-dimensional prosthesis.

There is a synaesthesia of ideas. An idea is an aggregate
of information accumulating mass by gravity. The gravity
of an idea is or isn't a metaphoric expression, depending
on how you look at it. In quantum mechanics, the observer
alters the observed. Physics has become meta-poetry.

THE CYBERNETIC HOLIST

" . . . any ongoing ensemble of events and objects which has the appropriate complexity of causal circuits and the appropriate energy relations will surely show mental characteristics."

— Gregory Bateson

Compositional circuits and textural gradations undergo
an existential transform, so that the Mona Lisa seems to
smile at you.

> That moment will live on in us forever.

Death is a casual evolution of ideas
among systems, with some ideas used as eyepatches.

A commune with nature. The landscape's ego. I was tossed out for
hoarding percepts.

●

The car had a mind of its own. He kept calling it his "baby,"
but he kept flooding the engine like he would never do to
his wife.

> His wife divorced him on the grounds of
> mental cruelty.

There are three of us in the room.
You, me and the room.
If you love me, don't leave the room.

> Haunted houses are residual mind.
> Mind you don't trip on the stairs.

The floor of Heaven.

> Extended metaphors are a homey stasis of mind.

●

Keep the elements out.
Turn the elements on.
You are a walking thermostat.
You sleep with the window open.
An idea comes in, and what do you do?
You sleep on it.

Why did you remove that plant from the corner?

He left home to go to college.

One frying pantheist into the fire.

●

Traffic centres, nerve centres,
intersections, traffic circles,
the communications tower, the bypass,
the learning complex, the transformers,
the failed transmission. The body of knowledge
driving one out of one's mind.

Descartes giggling on the moonlit cloverleaf.
No one's asphalt.
Mumbling the whole is larger ergo sum.
The ghost without the machines.

INFORMATION IS WHAT PRODUCES information. Quanta
defied or deified in the act of observation. You
can't get away with most of the information. The
propogations leave home and you can't take them
with you. The information will not enrich you as
a consumer analyst. There is information trapped
in stones that will remember you as you pass by.
In Minnesota this is known as stone-consciousness.
Elsewhere, they will say you are stoned. Meaning
you can take it with you, in the corporational
sense. Like Baptist Network Religion where you will
snipe the commies in Heaven. Corporational and the
incorporeal meeting of minds with the stone as the
State of the Art.

"The computers have no feeling."
"The computers have no feeling."
This is an error in logical typing.
This is an error in logical typing.
Confusion of the children with the parents.
The information leaves home without you.
How else could they see you from a satellite.
How else could they know where you are.
Information is what produces information.
You always did talk too much.
Electric engrams reshuffling dinner-settings
in an effort to get past the closed loops
of your mind. Nothing takes over.
There is mercury in the trees.
There is strontium 90 in the bones.

Auto-poeitic structures
are holographically replicative in ascending or
descending heirarchies.

A rose is a rose is a rose. . . .
Metaphor is an error in logical typing.
Cumulative errors in logical typing,
or meta-language layers, confuse the map with the
territory;
the word made flesh.
Murder for a higher reality.
A poetic license to kill.

The electrical impulses of a telephone wire are
not identical with the voice of a loved one, but their
gestalt matches the gestalt of the voice.

"A tear is an intellectual thing"
— William Blake

Numbers are informational transforms for the
"thing in itself." The correspondence of mathematics to
reality assumes an error in logical typing.
Map coordinates won't keep you from crashing into a tree.

"A language is a map of our failures"
— Adrienne Rich

Systemic convergence exhibiting structural
and component symmetries are epistemologically
transcoded as
"truth is beauty and beauty, truth"

Similarly Einstein thought an idea had to be elegant to be true.

Wordsworth's cottage is an aesthetic cyclotron
assisting in the ongoing search for subjective reality.

A BLACK HOLE IS AN IMPLODING space and a white
hole is an exploding space. The smaller variety
of these are 10^{-33}cm in diameter and 10^{-5}gm mass.
They honeycomb space/time. Bits of consciousness
superluminally traffic through these hourglass sin-
gularities in which time stops and re-emerges, con-
sciousness riding a Pegasus of reconfigured light.
The collapse of space/time at the waist of the hour-
glass is as inexorable as the flow of time outside
the hourglass. Rapids through which consciousness
hurries before resuming linear mirage. A timeless
hourglass, the grains of which are immaterial for
the instantaneous. Flickers of existential timescapes.

HALOES ARE BIO-GRAVITATIONAL after-images, the scorched
outline of intense thought. A leaf's aura will remain
projected on a ghost periphery even after the leaf has
been cut in half. That relation is haloistic. This mor-
pho/temporal resonance is sustained superluminally by
proliferation of black hole/white hole trumpets in the
sentience-ecology of the leaf. The halo fades as the
leaf turns its attention to the repair of its biosphere.
Three dimensional loyalty, the will to leave.

THE AURAS OF SAINTS are keenly visible at the point of
death. Ecstasy distends the quantum matrix of the body,
permitting light to breathe multidimensionally. Light,
eddying around the three dimensional, the scaffolding of
flesh, casts a negative shadow, blinding rather than
invisible. Ecstasy is effected by the constructive
interference of all bio-systemic waves. Destructive
interference produces idea/logical factioning, polarized
ideatic fields repelling and mutually annihilating,
comparable to the encounter of particle and anti-particle.

WORMHOLES IS THE CURRENT theoretician's term for
the timeless hourglass. Poetry is science with the
brains to know that you have to live with your
metaphors. The id is as monstrous as it sounds.
The hourglasses connect different universes or
different regions of the same universe. This is
hard to visualize, according to theoretical phys-
icists. Sensory topological conversions are ad-
visable, unless you are a worm. One commonly feels
that which one cannot visualize. Cogni-modal synaesthesia.

THEORETICAL PHYSICISTS ARE FOND of saying that
the fourth dimension is almost impossible to vis-
ualize. A pornographic despair as the eyesight
dwindles, the ageing scientist clutching at the
sensory genitalia, sans eyes sans teeth sans sans
everything. They would see an embrace if they could.
The obvious is always escaping them. The timeless
hourglass is hard to visualize, along with most of
the world's poetry, heightened states of consciousness,
good sex and the taste of apple pie.

THE TIMELESS HOURGLASS rides the
circuits of longing, tugs the slung desires.
The hourglasses wait in the core of solar starfish
splashed on fenders, are couched on the hammocks
of photonic gusts. You draw near like one eavesdropping
on teenage conversations. In this one you placed
a sliver in the limbic node of a tressed nymphite;
the grief grew into a splattered arabesque, her husband
memorized on tile. You are vigilant in these repressions
now, flowering into desperate learning. What fandangos
of lies shaping the backbone; you are older and you
rebound in the resilience of time. The hourglasses

trumpet gravities from the grave and from the cradle. They are timeless, opportunities with a second chance, like patient gentry lounging on the furniture, grails winking at you from a regenerate past.

BRAIN LITANY: Or, Overlooking the Existential Factor

"Can it be that any man has the skill to fabricate himself."
— St. Augustine

The brain is a network of connections of cells
It is not a connection of cells
It is a connection of information
It is not a connection of information
It is a connection of blue vases
with red flowers in them
It is not a connection of vases
It is a connection of living memories

" . . . when we think of coconuts and pigs, there are no coconuts
or pigs in the brain." — Gregory Bateson

where are they
where are the coconuts
where are the pigs

The brain is a network of behavioural potentialities
The brain is the mind
The brain is the central integrative role in human performance

where are the pigs
where are the coconuts

The brain is a compendium of holographic mechanisms
Help me find the coconuts Help me find the pigs
The brain is a neuro-physiological metaphor
The brain is an illusionist's exercise in Euclidean geometry
The brain is a vibrational amplifier for ambient field quanta
Find me the goddamned coconuts the pigs
The brain is a cybernetic miracle with a three ring
triune brain circus at its centre

The brain is an enchanted loom where millions of flashing
shuttles weave a dissolving pattern
I know I saw the coconuts
I know I saw the pigs
The brain is an evolutionary archaeological site
Show me those pigs one more time

The brain is a dance among three interconnected biological
computers
I saw the pigs
I saw the coconuts

The brain is a bicameral structure for playing
epistemological handball.
I know you have the coconuts

The brain is a reality structurer with lacrimal glands
The brain is an international casino for quantum indeterminacy
The pigs
The pigs
The pigs

When we think of brains, there are no brains in the brain.

The coconuts
The pigs
The brain is a psycho-biological tar pit *give me*
the bloody coconuts in an emotional jungle *you bastard*
or the brain is a macro-evolutional myth for the maintenance of
I'll bash the brain is an omnidirectional time machine
clogged with death consciousness

I could cry

Show me those pigs
Show me those coconuts

THE ABRIDGED CARTESIAN VERSION

I think, therefore I am.

When we think of the "I," there is no one in the brain.

Where am I?
Where am I?   etc.

THE PIGS AND COCONUTS were holographically encoded
in the universe. The brain was diversionary. Linguistically
duded-up to make it seem central, while the mind decayed
into orbits of hunger, diminishing spheres of return,
seduced to a lonely room with no fresh news. One mirror,
the face of god itself, the mad Narcissus.

      Entropy by language.

      A homely statis of affairs.

The God-in-hiding is negentropic. The pigs and coconuts
became less tangible as the pineal light of consciousness narrowed,
lighting smaller and smaller portions of the holoverse
plate. The image blurs. A dim recollection remains.
Ex-communication. When science becomes ex cathedra.
The bicameral voice shouts itself down.

      The pigs and coconuts were everywhere, right under
one's nose and with the tree in the forest. They were with
the rose in the holoverse plate. Riddles are not for
the god to hide behind.

      "You have a three-by-five inch hologram of a rose."

      "Where is the image of the rose in the plate?"

Where is the rose?
A hologram is an interference pattern of light waves on a plate.
Where is the rose?
A hologram is a temporal localization of field quanta.
Where is the rose?
A hologram is a virgin beam with accumulated experience.
Where is the rose?
etc.

Language is a ruse by a man who knows that riddles can be
taken seriously. The hiding of a man playing God.

The geo-somatic inebriations
caused this evening
the geo-somatic, trans-deducible
transforms of transforms.
Everything folds its arms, everything
folds like paper airplanes.
Ideas folded in flight.
The dream transform of branches.
Vision and the instantaneous
embodiment, the sky like a pallor, the sky like
a sky at the trans-dimensional depot.
The sky like three minutes and then like caresses
and then the synaesthetic pin-ball into the approved
chreode of belief. The body like a tacit
contraption. Touch the body.
Touch the unconscious. Look at the arms folded.
Look at the arms embracing, the topological
transforms of the idea becoming itself,
the manifestive lingering in the manifesto.
The door opens two ways says
the manifesto. Embrace of self or others, the folding
or opening of arms in time, says the time manifesto.
Time topologically folds; it is the corner folded
as you turned the corner, so you walked sideways
into her life manifested.
Where is the manifesto of the two-way street,
really, where are the buds opening into the

doors of weather. You have a picture of time
standing still in the middle of the two-way street.
You have the picture drawn on the paper airplane.
If you may not find it ever.
If you may not find it ever.
May you ever be lucky at the top of the ecological
clock, may you spin in the evening, geo-somatically,
with the inebriations of cause.

Gravity in a black hole crushes an object
to the vanishing point, and it reappears in a new
space/time coordinate.

Magicians use black holes as crutches, employing the
gravitational equivalent of the speed of light to
make things disappear.
A skilled magician will steer you towards an
orientation of black holes and, by first preparing
you in a bath of high speed thought interactions
will start you blurring in the spatio-temporal realm.
He sits back and lets the black holes do the rest.

A bad magician will not know where he's sent you.
This is why people are careful about falling in love.
Good magicians hear you coming out of apertures in the
air and see to it that you don't materialize
in a wall of disbelief.
You will appear to have come naturally.
Your life will appear a sequence of fortunate events.

Magicians are people who distort the space/time
fabric. They are controlled vortices in the
quantum foam.

If a magician accumulates the bio-gravitational
gestalts of disciples without releasing them now and
again, he will implode.
Bad magicians of this sort are infatuated with locality.

The flesh is weak is a warped reference to the
dangers of locality.

If people could be compressed to a size smaller than 10^{-23}
centimetres, they could disappear. This is a causal fantasy.
What in fact happens is
they become less noticeable and merge with zones of light.

No one knows what's missing.

"The most extreme form of nihilism would be the view that every belief, every considering-something-as-true, is necessarily false because there simply is no true world."

— Czeslaw Milosz

Interconnectedness of all things does not make things less lonely for the post-reductionist mind. The mind tries to create its landscape even as it is travelling through it. The unknown is no longer in God's hands, but under the jurisdiction of mind. The mind cannot trust itself, because it has been taught to doubt. To doubt and trust at the same time is like trying to defeat Heisenberg's Uncertainty Principle. You cannot be in two places at once; only God can. Heisenberg's Uncertainty Principle is tenable if you are faced with the uncertainty of an electron — but, if you are faced with the uncertainty of the meaning of existence, what you experience is infinite regress, perpetual anguish, and physical death.

The good old days; don't give me flak about
them; they made you what you are, God rest her
soul. Wallow in vistas of the superannuary and
new developments, but don't forget the perspective
that can respool you to foetus-like proportions shouting
mamma like an original myth;
                        the language was too soon;
he gurgled in symbiotics and before that
he mutedly wound around a molecule so effete in its
promise of things to come, that memory jostled like
a framework rooted to the earth, and transposing itself
into trans-dimensional curves that could only
come out a phoneme in a 19th century kitchen.
Repeated multi-dimensional re-wordings
of the same damned electron that
spun through the galaxies with the name "Humanoid"
stamped on it by a definiton of orbits. They weren't even
orbits; that was the nature of the curse or blessing depending
on how you looked at it. What did we have to say to the old
man? Thanks for a point of view? For choosing left instead
of right? For helping me think I'm upright instead
of downright, walking through earth like a diver suspended
to the gravity of another dimension? Leave him
with some illusions. Lucky.

Ex-postulate 1) *"There are known cases of such complete memory loss that the person experiences a second life, without direct knowledge of the former life."*

What did it matter what we remembered, something
about armies and hordes sweeping over the horizon of
memory until we were all flustered with the irrespective.
Such strange inverse topologies haunted us, meeting each
other as if in another universe we had met at
the same table and vowed to dream non-recognition
at the new beginning. It seemed ludicrous to go on like this
making pacts like erased blackboards; we couldn't even focus
on the outlines of the board too long without wondering
if we should throw that in too, like chips at a poker table
it would fatten the pot and who could carry
the winnings home, if luck came through, that crazy
lady we imagined to make the thing seem daring.
We left the room and no one recognized us and tableaux appeared
where the street should have been, like cut-outs in the air
we walked through spaces saying goodbye to each other. The
interim had been sad. We crossed invisible hands behind
        our backs.
like knotting interfaces of selves, and tilted our heads
towards the vacationy view. It always seemed the first dawn
of creation, when we left our homes to go towards
a job as distant as the space between one instant
and a déjà vu.
I don't know how many times I went down like that as the
poker game drew on, interminably, like the fiasco of
a nightmarish rule. And if you think that was funny
you should have heard my wife screaming my name
from which corner of the room I couldn't tell. Only I could
hear it, so I thought. Nothing would make me come to life
and own up to it. Their complicit silence was part of

the package. We had made that rule up, when was it?
Memory was another thing. We'd tell anecdotes in between
the poker hands that tied us to each other
with such sentiment, that it seemed for moments
the reason for anything.

Ex-postulate 2) *"Science is based on causality. Causality is based on symmetry breaks between past and future. Since time is relative to the observer, science is now based on probabilities."*

It seems like only yesterday the probable
was real. I love these semantic leaps that
people die making, going through loopholes
and pulling the borders in after them. They
then announce the aperture they just came
out of as cosmology. Time warp ingrates.
Painting themselves into epistemological
corners, finding elbow room in the mind's
crystal replicas and waving calipers like
wands. An anachronistic picture. Funny as
watching Heisenberg having it both ways
with the word "complementary" or Neils Bohr
with his yin-yang coat of arms while the
language giggles like brain gelatin throw-
ing up odds and ends for the cortical bait-
ing. I know a woman so lovely she lets men
talk and floats near them like time. They
stop what they're doing, symmetry break
upon symmetry break like piling train cars
and they learn nothing; except that they
thought a minute ago and now feel. She tries
again and again like the insoluble weather,
and they hurt on both sides until the heart
is emitted like residual mind grafted onto
wings and trees. It is a kind of ventril-
oquism. The magician's conjurings barking
at the wand. Most virginal. The naiveté

of self-belief. The making of oneself with-
out the luxury of knowing it. Uncredited
love consuming itself. Virgins in the corners
of the cosmos, scrubbing their language
like a pedestal.

THE PLATONIST AT VALPARAISO

Ex-postulate 3) *"All possible pasts, presents and futures are like different chan-
nels on a television set."*

The metaphor killed me. I lay down and rolled over
and remembered the sad birth notices I was
greeted with, and amorous remarks construed as
declarations to be taken to market and exchanged
for the pedestrian fish, the ovoid pears, the wife's
smug look transmitted back to me, like I had gone
out in public with my fly undone and had just
remembered it. Still, there was some charm
to the cruder analogies, as if one's romance had
been put to work at last, tired of swimming out
there among all those exotic fish you could
hardly collect you were so busy oohing and ahing
at their splendiforous eyes and you came back with
your nets empty. The sun was admonishing at about
5 o'clock and you could hardly wait to get out there
again, and you could put up with the wife's
nagging about your worthlessness about how José
down the road had raked in enough mackerel that year
to buy his wife a mother-of-pearl comb. Something about
the waves dancing and combing the sun spread on the
waters like a nymphad's hair. Droll expostulations,
what you had learned to expect, lying in bed, the words
failing you and dying to get back to the original.
You were at the service of something, on shore; you were
paying through the teeth and restoring yourself next day
on the still waters. The wife's snoring didn't
seem to matter so much and you thought of your
children, anxious to get to school, feeling
that any mishap was a reprieve from the dogma
of supper-calls. You might have been a great professor

knowing so much about grounded beauty, the young girls in
the class really appreciating it, mixing your lessons with
tips about net-fishing and tying it all in with the poetry
of the sun. What did the scalawag beside you know?
But you knew somehow that the wife was central, how you
would otherwise fade in the offing, in an indolence past
caring, forgetting to bail the water out of the boat, to
end up flailing among your favourite denizens; you would
save that for last, after the discharge of the only life
you knew, having promised your dying mother so much
conscience to walk the world with. And the wife
was a demonstration. You felt for her in an oblique
subconscious way. It wasn't her fault if she knew
nothing about fish, as anything other than
something to be plopped into a pan for stuffing into
the popular entrails. You would take her out in the
boat sometime, you once had thought. But now it would
hamper the momentum of natural events, the accumulated
days at sea, like an absorption, where your eyes would
skitter believably in a vortex of becoming, until the
boat was empty. To be sure, it wasn't really a plan;
and it would have been nice for her to have become
a mermaid, but she had fried fish for so long,
she had become terricolous. Each to his own,
in time.

MEMORY STORAGE IN PARADISE

Ex-postulate 4) *"As much as half the human brain has been removed without noticeable memory loss."*

It fooled everyone at first. But this was too much
what everyone had expected. It's like, faced
with that first valhalla of instinct you had to
figure it out in longitudes, recreation centres,
sewage systems. The dirty work had to begin, and our
children were angry with the slow logic we had accustomed
ourselves to, which would pass in time, we thought, as soon
as we got used to this cleaner air, the immaculate
assumption of the unworked — to be lived in with some kind
of gratis quotidian manner, but that wasn't it
exactly; it wasn't "manner" we were looking for or "way"
but some sort of leap into the formerly impracticable,
while keeping our pants and shorts on, when pants and
shorts weren't needed, if you see what I mean; the kids
spoke in vocables that better resembled the fences
of a new climate, or back of the mind yard. You could tell
by their throaty and birdlike paraphrasings that *fences*
was not what they had in mind. We knew they had the
ticket, but older, feeling responsible, we couldn't drop
everything and say *We'll follow you.* We couldn't believe
they no longer wanted food. And we were fed to death —
we thought we might feed ourselves out of existence
in the wake of some abstract luscious fruit we
couldn't get our simple fingers on.
Everywhere we went, things, like faithful mirrors (that's
putting it banally, which is hopeful), showered
plenty into their endlessly symmetrical mouths.
It seemed sadly delightful when we exhaustedly stopped
to watch; we felt like useless
thumbs; and we remembered poems

like affidavits announcing the birth of children;
such rude elementaries like cotton batting on
freshly filled molars. That was the image that came to
mind, an ache drowning itself, a remembered culture.

LETTER TO DING AN SICH: After the Fall

Dear Ding an sich.
I miss you.
I have looked through all the drawers,
found what maps I could find and they were
stamped *where is beloved Ding an sich.*
Physicalists mourn and search
in long cathedrals, dimensionally twisting
for the lateral apparitions of Ding an sich,
the old boy we'd hob-nob with in the schoolyard.
We try to be ourselves, to emulate like handing
down a story. It's the most we can convey of that
era. You should have been there, is the
common retort. You are like much
of a shadow, an adumbration of thought, like
a sense of old citizenry before a migration
to a land where the natives see height in terms
of width, and our new membranes, squint as
we may, retain a fore-image of something we
sometimes call platonic, but is too much
like the tang of a sunday sauce, lingering
on an equally platonic palatte. It is like being
in water, and the textures oscillating before
you grab them. Of course the fish are elusive.
They're not dumb, though we ascribe talents to them
in terms of extra bio-systemic dimensions. It fools
no one. Sleep is similarly bombastic. We pretend to
be scared of the ogres and precipices, and this is
a way of learning how to wake in the new land.
All in all, it was better with you. The delights are

various. Don't misunderstand! The logic, slow
as molasses from the charmed trees; it's like you'd
want to de-evolve into a fat white caterpillar, when
the air won't sustain wings. And now you'd have to
jump. That's part of the rules. You can't use
the convenient paraphernalia you thought would come in
handy for the trip.
     Mother would have liked it here. There are things
we kept secret, you and I. And no one is ever going to
come and get us. Remember how we used to pine
for that luxury? It was a game, just to keep us
from boredom. We thought they'd never find us in the
boiler room. They sure as hell won't. It will
get lonely until the cataracts grow in.

Ding an sich: The thing-in-itself

THE MATERIALIST'S DEMISE

Ex-postulate 6) *"Isolated material particles are abstractions, their properties being definable and observable only through their interactions with other systems."*
— Neils Bohr

It's like the vanished gold once you get to the Klondike.
You are left with your hard notions and the
commensurable pots and pans.
It would be enough to drive any materialist to open up
a saloon in the reparable town in the foothills, pandering
to what stray mongers arrive. You won't tell them about
the fiasco in the hills. The real abstractionists are still
prospecting, the beards growing, the mumbled songs petering into
the finger-snapping stream. They fall in love with trees
and slopes in five or ten years.
They'll manage a flimsy assurance of existing gold, to charm
you with a die-hard dream, but much like the child they
            never had,
it doesn't plague them all that often. The ambient mood is
what they really won't tell you about, hiding a cleft in the
slope by a weird declension of grammar. Leaning over the
saloon bar to tell the tourists, you also leave things out.
Let them go up and find no substitute for experience.
They'll be back at the real estate office in a month or
two, if they're your kind or they'll become those
damned angels up on the mountain, those transmutations
of gold, that sneak up on you like a glint of ore from
a four o'clock boulder, if ever there was one.
Your letters to Halifax talk about having the real thing,
the supply store got with the saloon profits.
The fact is you'd lie to anyone, because you see with your eyes
and can't believe in your own bad luck.
You even order a bride from the east. Her promises are as
pure as gold. You'll keep the talk to a minimum, the way

she hums those ditties into the wash.
You'd like to be surrounded by angels in a sense.
That's the kind of man you are.
Staking out everything and claiming nothing.

THE HOLONOMIST AT ALGONQUIN PARK

Ex-postulate 7) *"The brain is a hologram, interpreting a holographic universe."*

I used to live in a chinese box, but it got
so hot and stifling in there
that I had to reach out into the axiomatic,
encompassing three or more suppositions about
my nature. I couldn't keep disappearing.
I couldn't live in Nirvana, or on the road to
infinity. It was just dizzying. Blame it on
the body, I used to say, that homeostatic
nervature that lugs me back into the room just
as I'm flying out the window. "Happiness and its
untenability for extended periods," was a theorem for
excusing the body without mentioning it, so as not
to be rude. And who could kick a gifted catholic
horse in the face.
          The body pouted. It had its own reasons for
not getting to heaven until the dissipation
or full evolution of its carrier constituents of
will. Still, I wanted to get to the beach and romp
with Hanna among the blue waves, and she didn't want to hear
anything about the tracts of cognitive lineage
I had had to subsume just to tickle her fancy under
the undulations. She had her sights on the
blue fir on the escarpment so she could pretend not
to notice me doing it to her good. She had
marvellous double consciousness, orgasms without
so much as a nod of reflection. I envied this.
And I saw the tailing firecrackers tied to me, as
to a cat in the water. She had no problems with
digital sequence.
          I would try one more paradigm. That's what
I always said to myself and then I could concentrate

fully on the good times she chimed on about
as if there were no tomorrow. The waves of course
intermingled like informational waves gathering node-like
at her thighs. I would steal another glance of
course, just as I pinched her. The waves after all
had their own kind of beauty.
It was always two kinds of beauty, whereas Hanna was
always prepared to look the other way. I wasn't about
to propound a thesis on fickleness. Let's say her
nonchalance was exquisitely biological.
And I cursed that I was made a man.
I would tell her about that, back at the cabin,
between cool sheets, what with the furnished dialectic
refreshing as a closed system of considerations,
simple enough to achieve, ostensibly,
once the excitement was over.

THE CAROL OF *PRINCIPIA MATHEMATICA*

Ex-postulate 8) *"Res extensa, res cogitans."*

Who wants to be left out in the cold.
It's lonely out there, walking between one
christmas party and another, and I remember
a sophomore girlfriend shouting *you love
words more than you love people;* she might have
said *as much as people* and it still would have hurt.
She was a nice catholic girl with a regular analyst,
or as Descartes said "I think, therefore
I am," meaning, that everything
outside human reason is wet, vaginal, ugly,
full of stupidity and night. In fact, that's why
I left her; she had a Cartesian hot-tub at home
and steeped herself in it daily, just to come out
guilty about herself. But I was too romantic to be
a therapist and was too young to know that words
are of a different logical type than people. So I pitted
one against the other.
        I still remember the way she used to turn the lights
out when we made love, like an erasing, the bodies
perfectly "extensa," and we'd sneak into those delicious
subterranean zones that like flocks of
distant birds, nattered of completion, and yet were always
off to Capistrano. When would they come back? When we
unlocked the double binds? I read somewhere that the
light bulb is the male womb. I wanted it on. The light
of reason bringing us to a logical conclusion.
I felt bad about that, and am still training myself to
make love by daylight. It's an erroneous symbolic gesture.
But I'm of sacrament age, and am beginning to find out
that the folks at the christmas party are not an answer
what with the lonely hydrants, streetlights, bushes and the

myth-consumed fir fleshing out the corner by the hearth.
The word made flesh is an error in logical typing.
I didn't know that as a sophomore —
that I couldn't make things whole by giving them names.
And I hope her mind and body came together.
I guess that's all she was mad about. That I was
exalting a split very much connected to her menstrual disgust.
We never send christmas cards to each other at
xmas; a tacit salutation of having graduated from
something; a message of some maturing.
The deciduous by the hearth can't be worshipped into
the everlasting green.
She was a Spanish catholic.
She was so tortured she was always
beating me to one illumination or another.

OMNIJECTIVE NIGHTMARE

"Was there any place where I should not be prey to myself?"
                                        — St. Augustine

Ex-postulate 9) *"Rationality occurs after knowledge has been obtained
viscerally."*

But he usually thought the cart before the horse,
and sometimes the cart would sprout hooves
in his imagination and it was just as good, having
learned to create his reality, though someone would peer
over his shoulder and say, periodically, that he had
no choice about that either. Provisional theorems
abounded like foal over fences. No sooner had he
settled into the pretty gestalts of four or five
of them in a pretty configuration mimicking the
caress of his first wife, than they'd break up
and join the cranking aesthetic of the guy next door.
Realities re-assembling, before his very eyes.
He would reach out, the deer would come to eat, and
he'd think *work* and the scene would change like a dream.
Training might retain the scene; heightened states
worked at. Practice made perfect. And then he'd
slip into the pat assumptions that the food was
keeping him in shape for the job.
The visceral generally escaped, like the air that had been
around so long it could not help but be seen as
a viaduct for airplanes and things. The tacit was
great fun though, as if one had missed something
and was happy to be told about it, like the unconscious.
He looked at the family of electrons nattering about
on paper and it was like his hand and the warm vortex
it felt in the bathtub when he was six years old.
A science of that connection was not his field.
He didn't publish his guts, and someone didn't paint

their neuronal pathways.
Accidents would happen, and people would gather around them
like a car crash. A moment of exquisite junction, where
the human element met the mechano-morphic.
Descartes crashing into the horse. The dash of paint
on canvas that had swung round from a third arm
behind the painter. The unexpected. The soul
clambering up from the escape hatch, figuring the
air was distilled enough to kiss the patrons.
These were cheery moments called art, so irregular
they'd piss people off and send them into the
probabilistic. Sometimes they'd meet themselves
half-way as in a mirror. Matter and mind
would present what had often been left out:
a third. And they would stop and watch;
and wonder, and sometimes this would create
a theorem that was a live hare
before they started hounding it.

PROTO-NARRATIVE BREAK

HE'S GOT A VIRGIN HEART the way he struts his points of view between the latticed ideologies, conscientiously shutting them when he's through, leaving a note on the sill, correcting the geometries of his bones to conform to some preternatural vision hidden like candy under the wrappers of his sparking neural-calamities. Nothing would ever make as much sense to him as the vision he was puppeted to, as if he was a tree sublet to legs and arms, eager to mouth on about leaves and the arroyos of wind. He was a virgin among the odds; he touched himself like a maniac blessing, hurriedly moving in the somnambulance of his task to other bodies and his unwitting transferences charmed the air and became paradigms. These paradigms were like pups chasing him, wanting him to own up to them. He was so bogged down with the hungry mouths he hadn't fed as he was feeding that he was always being refused admission to reality, that plane of circumvented peace, creation, where he was co-creating.

THE COCKTAIL MARTYR

Ex-postulate 10) *"Magicians could make coins disappear if they squeezed their hands hard enough."*

But you just don't want to, do you?
You know you could if you tried, but you
just don't want to. That's always been your case;
afraid to snuff out half your loving world
by a gross application of intelligence, or just
by bearing down and bringing to bear all your
confections of stored accumulated etc.
And what if you did make them disappear
oh then they wouldn't believe you would they
even though they'd got front seats for the affair,
you know they'd call you a liar or pluck
their eyes out and deny having had sight —
they'd make out a new universe in which sight
was as remotely considerable as
cold germs from a passing asteroid rather than give
you credit for one more astonishment in the world.
It boils down to a failure of nerve, my boy.
Take cover if you will behind ontogenetic programming
you'd like to disown but find more kosher to
share out of courtesy. Matters of conscience are just the
right size for the mask at the ball. Everyone gets them
from the same curio shop and the comparisons
are analgesic to the knowledge that you could bring
the house down by removing your mask, say around
9 p.m.; once every five years you go naked, but you
don't want to make a habit of it; just how much
verve for the ornery you have must be kept a secret.
The legend of your life is worth that much.
It begins to dawn on you that something will squeeze
the life out of you with every passing year of

the suppressed fabulous: inversely proportional
to your refusal, and it doesn't get easier. You get lonesome
for all you could lose, as if you'd peopled your own
dollhouse and now the characters are all you know
of affective moments. Like charming yourself
into a cage of ribs, with you fluttering to get out.
You begin to feel medieval, with just your head poking
through the membrane of sky, and the body gutted to the
earth. How are they going to bury you like that, at
the very end. You'd like to hand over your eyes
like a passing comet, and right about then your body
is so much love from the waist down, that nothing
can make it disappear. Just see where your
sentiments get you.

Ex-postulate 11) *"The schizophrenic is a failed magician."*

So torn with divided loyalties, his left brain
and right brain like two halves of a broken wand;
he'd bring them to his wife and make entreaties.
By the time she'd parcelled chores and dinnertime
and time for him, the kids tucked into bed she'd
be scatter-brained too. Another magician might do
the trick; a romance hunt for whoever could fit the
pieces together, alchemical rituals of candle-light
and music, synaesthesia with ideas fondled and revived,
made to come alive as if no one had ever understood
you before. In fact, you were saying things you didn't
know you had in you as you held hands across the place-
mat at Harry's Diner, as the new woman stared incredulously
and needful. Charmed I'm sure. Such magic, and you tossed
the word around to your friends. She was "magical." It
was okay. You were in love, free to commit all kinds
of gaffes, stumbling into the watercooler, misplacing the
Hampton Account. The boss would overlook it. You were
in love and everyone slapped you on the back as if
you'd gotten maternity leave from hell and the schizo-
phrenia of scattered deadlines, disparate trips,
confused messages, the conscience squashed between career
and meaning well. The affair would last for a while
until you lugged it into the mundane, as you always did.
It seemed your curse. You'd love, and by that act throw
someone to the day to day furies. Five years later
someone else would say "you weren't to blame." Exoneration,
as good as grace. Each mistress talked of timing, as if
hunger made us all idiotic. Well, who could get used
to happiness as a way of life. We were all in the
same boat and now and again two would swim out for

a tryst on the atoll. The question was always, "what ever happened to those magic times we had?" It was easy enough to say we were out of sync. Mind you no one ever made a study of how to get into sync, as if that would disrupt the natural flow of things, ruin the magic. It was that craven. The sacred drawn up to the chin like blankets to fend off the bogeyman, who probably just had sweet choppers; who wanted to kiss you and plant a rose on your head.

THE PATSY OF THE MANY WORLDS THEORY

"When you lose your mind it's great to have a body to fall back on."
                                        — ad for Calvin Klein Jeans

Ex-postulate 12) *"The reality we experience in ordinary states of consciousness is due to the constructive interference of the dynamic phases or actions associated with each of the indefinite number of coexisting universes."*

Then how do we modulate experience into
the obvious patterns, he asked, the word *obvious*
catching in his throat as though he'd always
known he'd pushed redundancy to the outer limits
by failing to celebrate the moment. And the moment
would catch up with him at the moment of death,
all the copies of the universe he'd invented
not fantastic enough, and he'd die the way
he lived, expectedly.
His brain should have been more active without
assuming a pen would drop to the floor if he
dropped it. All the neighbours' backyards looked alike —
he'd had a hand in that. If he hadn't been so
sentimental they might have changed before his eyes.
He wanted everything the way it was, and everything
obliged. Side-road after side-road looked alike,
with worthless modifications of shrubbery, an added
songbird, a dead raccoon ahead of him, the friend
waiting for him at the rented cabin, much as he
had imagined. The extraordinary, the really frightening
behemoth stomping out of the hillside; he knew that
would panic him, but the body would stay calm. It had
more intelligence in its little finger than in all
his tiers of thought. His body was intelligent and his
mind a conundrum rolling up and down his vertebrae like
a ball-bearing. Somewhere, someone imagined greatly;
and this might allow his body to go to the lions

peaceably. Oh how he longed for that, the body swatting
the mind aside to greet the behemoth fearlessly.
He'd fantasize this at a good remove, envying his
body and generating cancer cells. It was self-hatred
pure and simple. Total intelligence was out of
place. He had a wife in the city, a paper to read,
colleagues to indemnify the normal. He'd kill the
body rather than let it mortify him. Such was the
nature of love in the colonial orbits of the cortex.
As much as could be imagined, was as much as things
would ever change. And there were multiplications of
boredom, so that they ganged up on you at any
given time, on a day like any other.

Ex-postulate 13) *"The brain is in the mind but not all of the mind is in the brain."*

Some of those little buggers get away and become full-
fledged notorieties of interpersonal relations with
tree bark. Some of it spills over the chalice of the body
and anoints the greener grass of disbelief. More than
meets the eye. Conquistadors used to shove the black-skinned
slave ahead of them as they made their way into the
jungles. This was done to surprise the light-skinned
cannibals who had never seen a negro. The shock wore off
pretty fast and the arrows would start arriving on
time. One should always throw out the arbitrary bone to
distract the carnivorous self, projected or contained. The
fully preposterous, like Jacqueline dipping her fingers into
the brandy and flicking the drops at your face in the middle of
a conversation about French semiotics; to call it a good
sense of humour would be like calling a meteorite additional
mass for the earth. That lady had brains. And made men feel
silly and self-contained. Well someone had to erect buildings
and calculate the angularities of cornerstones. As we were
talking her kid used to slide down the banisters as if there
were no tomorrow. And it was tomorrow that gave us our
sense of symmetry by which we could construe the heart and head
and feet. And sometimes a variable would strike us in the
ribs like an arrow suggesting we were the left hemisphere
to their right. We would look down at the trickle of blood
from the wound with such mundane rejoinders as *I see they're
using painted arrowheads this month.* That was the way we added
meat to the bones of the empire. Consummately, with such little
imagination that the shrunken heads were just satires compared
to the reality of things.

Ex-postulate 14) *"Every particle in the universe possesses consciousness."*

Once I told her that it was all over.
Her personal suspicions all verified and
cast into the light of day left no
mystery intact; the sequin dresses, masks,
dictums conveyed by mother at the lace dresser
had gone by the side of truckers, goons,
blackjack villains; true democracy was as
aesthetic as a stratosphere without a loophole.
I had tried to leave messages and had hinted
with squirrely eyes; what, I said, did
you think were the flashes of morning about?
What was the be-all and end-all of your passion, if
not a kiss hooked to communions that would sew our
love in deprivations of place, time and ignorant
planetoids. She would hear nothing of it — gearing
herself up for charades of woe-begotten affairs.
I was left with the customary particles, from which
I would clone royalties, hierarchies of fleshed
beatitude. It was given to me to have two arms, two
legs and have that much in common with symmetries
who were right-handed or left-handed and had one
foot in the grave. Next time around I would sew
jellyfish and bluebells to my exoskeleton
and waft upwards on the grace of a fading notion
and land squarely in the blind spot of two lovers kissing.
Fat chance. Every new beginning was a cranked up
polemic about the elementaries of metaphor, about how
the flesh was canvas and the lips, cloud-trumpeters.
Oh, you know! the rigmarole of the better half —

Janus with a straight face and the near annihilation of opposites. What would I want to go and do that for? you might well ask, knowing choice was of that other world, and having to ask just the same.

LAZARUS, THE INERT

"To try, on the other hand, to understand and deduce the human from the sub-human or brute mind is to try and fit the lock to the key instead of vice-versa; it is to seek to illuminate light by darkness."

— Rudolph Otto

Ex-postulate 15) *"Consciousness is a fundamental property of protoplasm."*

Sure; and alertness is a property of bone marrow; still, it's
nice — sea creatures in their vesicles of gelatin brewing
thoughts of Danton and the French Republic, communicating
by sub-oceanic resonances combed by seaweed under Île de Ré,
raised barometrically by sand and wash and tans, connived onto
blankets, residues humming in Citroëns all the way to Le Havre,
waxed in the winds, scuttled against high-tension wires,
particles swimming and grafted by elements and washed into
a home receiver, *voilà!* the admixtures of the planet's
opinions on trans-temporal events. Ho hum, how cosy. The
possibilities roll over like puppies doing tricks that
shake even grandpapa from his world-weary somnambulance.
The vitalists are wrestling logical positivists in the
backyard under the laundry flapping like old epics against
the fashion of ideas. Once in a while I awake to a standard
mode of popular feeling, grooming itself like a poodle fed
up with handling and fuss — a hairy little narcissus come
this far on flattery and ready, it thinks, to meet the
unmown grasses and the wilds. He'll be back squealing
at the screen door in an hour, happy to be divested of any
illusions, dependent on the house, its mindful fabrications —
plenty of ideas, new rubber mice, plastic bones, jingling
latex balls. Bounded amusements. Forays are bracing. It was
not without good reason that grandpapa was mileaged into
a rocker by a taunting and punitive world; excursions that
bunted his heart into easy inertias and local congratulations
like patting the cat. And now the protoplasmic was delightfully

invested with home-grown potentia, as if life had been
discovered on Mars, as if natives were reported to have used
gold foil as placemats on the oystered beaches. No use
going that far. The pond behind the house wanted your feet
webbed in return for historical thoughts zeroing into the
weeds confusing your musings with gadflies and muck, all
      reporting
back to the gelatinous brain that grew into the pond monster
that would walk into the house one night and want to know
more about the French Revolution. You'd walk out there
and feed it piecemeal with such obdurate facts, symbiosis
that kept you writing poetry in the house, like a governorship.
Eventually and good the lines would drift through the
screen door like existential creditings, convening in the
moonlit yard with the aquatic and linguistic meeting half-
way, with you safely out of it, autonomous and waiting
for breakfast.

NARCISSUS: Auto-Programmatic

Ex-postulate 16) *"Consciousness controls the bio-gravitational field."*

Consciousness controls the bio-gravitational field.
You run the pond, the cat's-tails, eddies,
amphibian motorists, dragonflies and the landing
strips sheaved blue, the air dome serenaded,
temperature inhalations of citizenry. Attention.
Intersecting patterns orchestrated in a glance.
Buying toe, ear and pancreas concerns, endemic
by the pineal light, a white angel in your brain,
projecting love; the scanner
lights on anything love-rife.
Consciousness controls.
You elevate the ecology of feeling, you pin the tail
on the donkey, this time me, but every so often
the embrace fits the scarves of feeling, and we swashbuckle
down the avenues, heart to heart.
Consciousness controls. The heart, today, is consciousness
where you placed it, moving it around, safe-kept; codger,
I have the secret, implant kisses, your field
your eddies. Emotionful, resting on mine,
relaying, piggybacking, millions of atoms congratulating
encounters, exchanging spinal handshakes while we kiss.

Ex-postulate 17) *"Atoms are formed by interactions between vibrational patterns."*

Was there nothing to be salvaged by the unexcepting
principles of the universe. Mother's kiss sufficiently
tickling the rough underbelly of the soul;
and she gave us language and the ability to differentiate
between good and bad, which as we know are now forming
a vibrational pattern and intersecting into this confusion
we now call emotional paralysis. And now we turn to the flowers,
small trumpets that shoot our abstracted versions of
fresh and subterranean axiomatics as if we'd ignored
under our feet all this time what would nurture us like a sleepy
and freshly awakened saviour. Oh to ride the vortex of
                informational
luggage like Pecos Bill riding the cyclone, ignorant and
spontaneous with his gutsy yells flaking over the hillsides
and towns and arriving like queries in the noggins of the
hoi poloi. Oh to step out of the symmetries once and for
all, even though the mathematical constraints kept
feeding us.

The bees didn't like the harbour; its salt air, anathematic
and preponderous; the bees in the bonnets fared better
atop the ladies and their finery, strolling with parasols,
talking in twos or threes, amused by inveigling the sailors
on deck who leaned over the side to graze their eyes on
landlubbers, while their elbows nosed carbuncularly towards
the Cape's latitude. No place for the land-beholden; nothing
but crates and sacks of grain and sapless flowers for a bon
voyage. Ecologies bruting each other. The bees, inebriated
with misdirection and memorized dances banged on the
moorings like a word trying to find its sentence, skimming
every inch of the cluttered strangeness for clueful symmetries;
they'd bump fuzzy brows into a map, a picture, a taste of
shadow lugging a holographic bunched feel for honey like a
fading notion. Stray bits of irrelevant but interesting
carcass met them like untimely fancies gone sour with panic.
The boat too would flunk out on an atoll carrying its
mandates and perplexed religions, nubbing the beach-heads
like a severed instinct. But for now these two oblivious chunks
of the world's intent swatted or stung each other crazily.
The kids sat on the crates and lapped up the funny incongruities
of the desperate meeting on their peripheries. They too
would be bagged by an idea, dragged aboard and forced to
watch fates unspooling like foods they hadn't asked for, but
were compelled to ingest, like time, like an epic to
which they were stunted adjuncts. They couldn't care less,
until mamma said during the storm "don't cry" and that would
be enough to make anybody cry, feeling for the adult, sentiments
they were fed like slabs of beef as the days stretched into
weeks and months. What did they know of beginnings and
endings.
Meanwhile the bees cubbed the cauliflower elbows of the sailors
whose scrutable eyes checked lust off like rosary beads on

the hems and lace dragging the wharf. They were trying to
        imagine
the worst for someone while the bees banged into brown roseates
mistaken for a hive and fizzled in the jumbling sun. It was an
erotica of impossible junctures, touted in the universities in
Lisbon as irony but stamened here on the child's flowerhead like
a branding iron, like gentleness on a spit, like the fleshed
needs clambering the surreal with the tears so advocated by
mother, cooling, cooling.

Another objective constant, clung to, a desperate
stronghold where the word-spinners would gather
en masse and call the walls a necessary evil. The walls
were so crusty you could poke your finger through them
and befuddle the merchants at their bazaars. You could
twiddle your finger all you wanted and they'd pay no
heed, their backs turned to your tomfoolery and their
eyes peeled. Well, a flag, a barracks and a commissary
were a must for poets too. They needed a place to
call home;

      a pragmatist would walk through their gates and
they'd say, "Oh what you see is an illusion; we live
from oasis to oasis, eating the transitory fruit. You have
stumbled upon us by the providential resonances of all
things at the cross-roads you call *a garrison,* because names are
holy or necessary evils depending on which side of our
mouths we are speaking." The risible dudes. The women
laughed uproariously outside the concocted walls, within
earshot and adaptive enough to make the muse look like
a fossil. They worshipped two mouths but then they had two
brains, one ambulatory to the other. The poets took this
verisimilitude as gospel symmetry. The worse for them; they
babbled like confused rabbis, wifish about the word
of God, its errant mysteries, when the women married the
pragmatists instead of them. Back they went to hammering
Le Mot Juste into gold so thin it wasn't of use to anyone.
There they were, quite exposed, with no walls, putting on
airs of abstraction, raising the objective constant up
a notch with every failed proposal, modelling Le Mot Juste
like spring fashions, waltzing around with variously
coloured haloes. They grew beards and were always too young

to start again, muttering, "Things are not what they seem, things are not what they seem." The gold coins glinted at the bazaar, and no one took them for what they were either. That was the irony of it.

TRINITARIANS

Sacralization was his magnum theme.
Reappointing his mother virgin of the world;
maps and charts strewn everywhere and out of
his head a bird lambasted out and returned
in threes, arriving one day as reptile,
mammalian and cortical brain, one day as father
and son and holy ghost, as id, ego and super-ego,
as male, female and high-wire act. Tireless;
the language gutting in his mouth like a fire,
rekindled and tooled into forging itself with itself,
like the brain inwardly staring, staring with the
tiny saint in him screaming "Don't give up," "find me,
find me." Recursive auto-erotica. His arms like
water slides he dreamt would plop him into the
spirited grasses, uncarnal and coastered to the
earth like a boyish seraph. Letters arrived from
similar pariahs of grief, compared notes for somatic
conversions into light, casebooks of virginizings,
micro-particular and versified. The latest articles
on auras meted out to the mondial chimp dialling
trans-dimensionally to the watch-dogs of a better
life, though the word *life* began to be meaningless
at this point; that which to escape *from* and escape *to*.
Again, the language tongued itself, double-bound to
need and the contempt for need.
         He operated on good faith.
When all was said and done, this could be said of many of us.
No one was truly evil. No use in complicating
things. We'd check off the messianic and the ignorant
and wash in between like soaked angels, vertiginous,
articulate but weighted by the apperception of wings.
If we could live a paradox by the brute force of will,
imagine ourselves devils and ply towards heaven.

Not in the books. We remembered *The Waste Land* and grew
nostalgic. Oh to be that simple, simply to have lost
the grail. But to be your own God and to have invented
the world badly; that was too much. Funny that the
body looked like a cross when you spread your hands
out. You had to get away from such nonsense and you
whipped and whipped until the language fled the
mind like a beaten carcass. Then you'd forgive it and
mull it in your mouth like a sacrament. The pores
gnashed angrily at the neutral air, shouting it down,
out of plain old love.

v. THE FUTURE WITH A HUMAN FACE

"God is thus not absolute, he evolves himself — he is evolution. Since we have called the self-organizing dynamics of a system its mind, we may now say that God is not the creator, but the mind of the universe."

— Erich Jantsch

"It is impossible to give oneself to an anonymous number. But if the universe ahead of us assumes a face and a heart, and so to speak personifies itself, then in the atmosphere created by this focus the elemental attraction will immediately blossom."

— Teilhard de Chardin

"The universe talks to itself, but people talk to people."

— Octavio Paz

ODES TO THE JUST SOCIETY

"And I suppose there are still some Christians who could say what a sacrament is."

— Gregory Bateson

I

RE-SACRALIZATION OF THE WORD. The word made flesh, not a code, a transform for the *Ding an sich* — Eden buttonholed in a concept — The Nordic Duel of heart and mind, the pump cerebralized to fuel an engine, between cranial plates. Trinity. Not semiotica, the glorification of the meta-fiction, the overnight god on the Canary Islands, the pale namesake of the scorching truth back home. And all for the betterment of Man, God-killer, systemic altar with harmoniums called efficacies, state-funded catechisms for the perfect system here on earth; Protestants with gestalts kissing — and the mini-gods, the Bishopry of Jung, Heisenberg, Prigogine, the Dancing Wu Li capitalists, the psycho-biological trinities, the neuro-cerebral conduits for the Holy Ghost, the quantum leaps to the land of free will, where everyone is in control, where everyone is *in* control, everyone within his rights, rancour systematized, the runaway psycho-chemically quelled. We have a drug for this, for the seeing of God, for the peaceful sleep, for the constructive use of your free will. The system is complete, innocence at the meat-grinder, and at the other end, the subjugation to a God without eyes.

For an idea does not caress.
Gestalts do not embrace.
Myths are not sanctuary.
People are not gods.

And when you talk to yourself out of madness:
it sounds at first like yourself, until you hit
upon the one word in your tired lexicon that
means "gentleness," and out of it comes the only
evolution, *hope,* and out of supreme anger comes
compassion for yourself, the miracle, that there
are two in you, and one must pray to the other.

2

THE WORD *GENTLENESS,* you mull your body in it like
a sacrament. You are in the fundamental particle
left like a corner in the madhouse. The one word
your brain could not touch, your arms up like a child
mouthing *mother* to the dark, but your brain has
scavenged her too, and you caress the word like a relic,
gentleness, gentleness. Suddenly it does not
seem like a meta-fiction, a transform, a code — it is
a board adrift with you in the ocean of your Godness —
you are marooned from the state, the sisterhood, the art,
the humanists. You have sacked every temple with your
need, and the word *gentleness* bobs on the waters of
despair, and you do not dare to call it
a mytho-cultural product. There is the word made flesh —
there the truth, the absolute you scoffed at; your
relativism drifts under you like a broken net, and you
believe the word *gentleness,* and you are grateful
and if you are not an animal, if you have learned
something you thank something other than yourself.
And you do not call it history, culture or bravery.
You call it God, fleshed in the word, *gentleness —*
and you are cured of the notion of many realities.

THE LEFT BRAIN AND RIGHT BRAIN playing musical
chairs, rapidly like a rat on a rat wheel, chasing
its own tail, almost within grasp of a mouthful,
Utopia. Priest and confessor changing places, screaming
restlessness, memory dangling like an earring left
in the quick change. Wave and particle, myth and reality
concrete and abstract with the projected self at the side
of the tennis match shouting *Love, Love,* the semiotic
code. To control and surrender, to be schizophrenic and
find the lover who loves schizophrenia. But it is not
called disease, no one is to be diseased —
we are acceptably schizophrenic until "self-actualized."
Our virtual selves, our actual selves, the virtued self,
the virtual particle of self, so small, so ideatic,
it cannot caress you; it is like invisible light. You
are pale, albino, basking in the light of yourself.

•

TO BE OMNIPRESENT, a system of gestalts, systems
that are non-hierarchical, not one system stronger than
another but owing to the synergy of the parts, the selves
worshipping the larger self, the actualized individual
beholden to the actual system, which cannot be *man* since
that is oppression, which cannot be *woman* since that
is regression; a system whose rosary is
"omni-directional, multi-level ethics, recursive meta-
fictions, trans-mythopoeic realities" — words that mean
nothing, which we suckle for meaning, for we would spit
out meaning ungratefully if it offended the "self."
We shall celebrate the number *one,* we will overcome
digital sequence, we will absolve the garden for the
differentiation of gender. We will correct God, since we
invented him badly. What is this loneliness? What is this
loneliness we have learned to call self-sufficiency —

why do the words change and not the meaning, the hunger,
the hunger we are not quite prepared to call "normal"?
Are we not strong enough? Hail *tomorrow,* hail evolution,
hail oh system of co-evolving selves, hail e-volitional,
hail oh snake eating its own tail!

4

THE YIN YANG SYMBOL HAS a line curving through it like
a snake; it is the lonely snake between nirvana
and hell; it is man, or woman dreaming its two sides,
lonely for its own tail, dreaming auto-erotica. It is
Heisenberg dreaming of how he wants particle to be
wave and wave to be particle. It is Germaine
Greer wanting man to be woman and woman to be man, it is
the Shell executive wanting a home in the country and a
home in the city, it is the artist dreaming of the purity
of his motives along with public acclaim, it is the
average citizen trying to be humble when called to the jury.
We shall go one way or the other, we shall annihilate
particle with anti-particle, with a fusion of total
aggression — we shall muster up the face of God with
self-destruction, by going totally one way we shall
come out the other side — and to meet God, we shall
pretend we are Gods, with no other manservants before us.

●

*"If the nature of reality is itself holographic and the
brain operates holographically, then the world is indeed, as
the eastern religions have said, maya: a magic show. Its
concreteness is an illusion."*
                                        — Marilyn Ferguson

LOOK DOWN AT YOUR ARMS, THE ILLUSION that wants to
embrace. If the flesh is an illusion, you are better than
Protestant, you are Luther broad-jumping to *maya,* because the

flesh is weak, so weak it must be ruled by the mind. Turn
the flesh into idea, the word into symbol. We shall bring
heaven to earth or leave earth, or we shall be here and not here —
anything but to humble yourself before your limitations.
The price you pay is work, is the state's ethic, the price
you pay is joylessness; you stare at every illusion and
you scream *reality!* give us the hierarchy without the
hierarchy, the Princess shouts: the pea is giving her
sleeplessness, twelve mattresses or twelve holonomic levels
down, or twelve meta-levels down, down past the Jungian level,
the Freudian level, the physical level, the mentalist level,
the organismic level, the existential level — *there* is the pea,
the fundamental particle abstracted, the quark of our nature,
the paradox that will not sing, that does not love the mind
that wants your heart, that says: *accept the mystery,* and
you answer "what is unknown will shortly be known," and you
lose sleep over it. They bring in more mattresses. It's no good;
they are only ideas. There is nothing between you and the reality
of your pride.

5

THERE ARE MANY GODS to go through before you meet him.
It takes ten, twenty, fifty years. All one's dreams
should come true; it is faster that way. There are those
who stall, who are not "self-actualized"; the actual self
will burn itself in sacrifice — the state hurries you
to God and does not know it — it banks on placebos
of self-reliance, professional outlets; it sanctions
mini-gods like feminism, macho, the arts, child care,
roots — the altars of the self are Disneyland. Pray you
do not use them all, pray the illusions do not run out,
may your dreams not all come true, which I would not
wish on my enemies, that which is either the mercy or the
wrath of God.

•

YOU DO NOT BELIEVE IN YOURSELF ENOUGH is the voice
of the state. In Italian the word *Dio* has the word
io in it. God and I — two in you. Which the
Protestants have taken literally, meaning *one and the same,*
made with the alchemical, pride, the elected, those who
show the way. No, I do not believe in myself. It would be
        ungrateful;
that is why I am not always sure about my rights, which
is why I thank the discourteous, why I needed someone to write
for, a woman to work for, which they have called *romantic* because
self-sacrifice is out of vogue. The pedestals are scrubbed clean.
The regendered Gods are pedestrian, and everyone sneaks
a peek at the vacant pedestals, and *dreams,* which we
shall now call *fantasy;* here is reality, the empty pedestals
and the empty polemic. The pedestals are clean — shall we
transcend, shall we transcend ourselves and yet be ourselves?
Shall we have our cake and eat it too? Yes, it is the
American dream with german idealism thrown in,
to be God and yet to worship a God,
to be independent and yet submissive,
to be a man and to be a woman,
at precisely the same instant.
To be God. Please God.

I

GOD IS IN EVERYTHING, therefore nothing is evil says the literal mind, therefore there should be nothing to be afraid of, and hence no guilt, says the wishful thinker, still guilty over what he has not done that day. Let us be responsible to ourselves yet forgive ourselves nothing, and therefore let us look at compassion and find only the dutiful around us. The peace that passeth understanding is in the forgiveness when there is no reason to forgive, but the conscience is reasoned into motor areas and language areas and pineal nodes projecting consciousness and they have localized free will, and your decisions are gloved hands that will not handle particles. You will forgive, only by a supreme act of faith, totally arbitrary. You get no help here, you get no help unless you are caught in the act of consciousness by God. He is non-localizable. He is everywhere and nowhere, another paradox you will see-saw on, because you are a mentalist, and your emotions are in John Calvin's locker. He has the key. He has swallowed it and has gone to micro-hell.

2

BUT WE ARE THE AGENTS OF GOD, we do God's work and are privy by our good intentions, says Calvin, says the just society. We see or try to see God in everything — the "immaculate perception," we are optic in our search, it is the English love of the microscope — when there is no particle of matter smaller than the heart. How can you see Him without feeling, how can you feel without forgiving, and yet you cannot forgive what is not manifest to you. It is your destiny to look for what is looking, St. Francis said — but he meant "look" as metaphor. And you are literal-minded. You are in a Protestant country where seeing is believing.

CONNOTATIONS HOLOGRAPHICALLY OVER-LAYED to produce the interference node, the nugget of beauty you polish with your optic nerve, meaning coalescing from the termini of dissipitive cells called eyes and noses; shall we call them "humans," a protracted guess, theorizing "no" farfetchedly. Semantics? Hierarchy-haters, these latitudinal holists bunting themselves in God with reflexive contextuality. And God will see us, diaphramming our observing with laughter, like birds natting on our heads. Shall we serialize the randomness of that? How ignoble is it? Or is pigeon-shit ecologically gracious too? How is the brute beast to be wondered with, once become? How be primitive and Crusoe? How slice the gelatin of brain so it is east and west and meets, Heisenberging paradox with a third eye in the middle, lasering truth omnisciently and apparitioning the tuna sandwich on the kitchen counter; how to be writer and the character, created-creator? How to co-evolve two brains with the broomstick of will?

1

THE FUNDAMENTAL PROPERTY OF THE UNIVERSE is mental, not material. Models of reality are workable or unworkable depending on faith. Loci are reachable by Cartesian plotting because the mind expects to get there. Airplanes stay up because people expect they will. Structural erosion of aircraft results from the quantized volitional fields, interacting and reaching event nodes in the snapping of a wing bolt. Every particle in the universe possesses consciousness. Aggregates of quantized energy have greater causal potential, as do autopoeitic or self-renewing systems such as humans or ecologies. The weather and the spiritual disposition of those aboard the airplane corroborate in an event matrix. The volitional systems involved are discrete and in over-lapping gestalts, but the consideration of both is as impossible as the violation of Heisenberg's Uncertainty Principle. You cannot be in two places at once. A knowledge of all proximate volitional systems at the time of the bolt-snapping is impossible. Inspectors at the crash site deduced a mechano-morphic failure. The brute facts of destination are left to the human heart.

2

WILL IS CONTINGENT ON FAITH. Every quantum quiff, every particle interaction, every quantum transition is mobilized by the ineffable attraction of existence, the irreducible sympathy of particles for other particles, selectively . . . the inherent participation in larger systems. The will not to participate is no will. Faith is a priori to existence. Aberrant particles or aberrant consciousnesses in an entropy of faith reach extinction. Errant sympathetic attraction of systems, microcosmic or macrocosmic, results in dissolution of energy. Human systems seek to perfect themselves, to originate volition, to assume the will not to exist; an experiment peculiar to humans, to reach through the noösphere, to stop the clock that keeps their time, to overcome paradox by an act of will. Naturally, they assume everything is their fault. The wing-bolt coming off the aircraft is their fault along with every failure. It is the worst entropy. The spirit in antipathy.

III

HEARING THE BRIDEGROOM'S VOICE

"The inwardness that responds to value, that is both faculty and realm of human entirety, is known as 'heart.' This does not mean the life of the emotions as opposed to that of the mind; the heart itself is 'mind,' but it is evaluating mind, not merely mind obedient to the norm. It is mind warmed and moved by value toward value: mind as Eros-bearer."

— Romano Guardini

I am a dangerous man.
I know what I know —
justice has eaten me out like corrosive
living, my sacred metaphors have been lived in
by so many that the denotative remains
like the crude tracks of angels, like the mythology
after the numen has packed its bags,
and though I rue that lost ether,
I scavenge topology like a mudfish
ready to sacralize every mote by the brute
force of will, the dumb attraction to God,
that is graceless, instinctual to good, gloved.
I have visions befitted to a pasture, mulling
the sacred sun in an ensemble of beasts
and petals. There are no words
for that silence I crave like a brother sewed to the
underside of my skin. Bathetic and superluminal
is my true self. Citified, I arsenal my words
for the unquestionable, for, really, my heart
would have only one answer, no good for lifting
chairs or writing cheques. I am a deconstructivist
with the throat of a lark. Ridiculous as it looks
I market the tragedy. I try to find angels
in micro-trajectories, and the heart emblazoned
on the Janus-faced mysteries. It is absurd, and I will
tell all while the young girls lap ice cream
with as simple a reprieve as the day off from school.

World, require a beauty unafforded by me, that I
cannot afford, but could lie in with the
cortex round my skull like a serviceable

halo, historic, like a fading grudge.
Dangerous; like a heart electrified to life,
my silence inverts,
and accounts for everything, like a prayer
beached and stripped for light.

o

YOU ARE HOOKED ON SURRENDERS, you were made for it, your worshipping, practised on women, principalities, models of cognition, stroking the flanks of your legend, pausing on moon-lit nights with the photographable. It is love you wanted, not ethno-historic sheen and eroto-Floridian memories. It is your texture of love. It is your smile you were looking for, not the superannuation, the cottage, the tour. You sold yourself to get that smile from others. It was the smile before the poem, in the caress, it was the spine of ontology in everything you did, it was *mysterium* flexing a muscle, it was grace alluding to itself, its terminus and offspring. It was paradox, lived before duality.

o

HOW CAN YOU TELL THEM IT IS GOD they want; the drive is God-lust, stereoed, diapered, fuelled, catechized to liberation manuals, editorials, bedsheets, mortgaged. They exhaust you on their way to God, and you, like a fool, can be anything, a liberator, a macho, a poet, a father, a brother, a teacher, a hope. And you oblige them. You are the means, their expiation, you fulfill all roles away from home. Your heart is green and blue from travelling. You ask every woman to let you rest. She will say anything to get away from home.

o

HE SAW TOO MUCH. He asked to have his eyes plucked out, to be sequestered, before the Mary, who tempered him to tolerance, gentling him. On the streets he scavenged for purity and saw only those who shared ignorances, blissfully. He tried going back, weightlifting, young girls, bandying wit with feminists; he sat in homes, periodically, playing house, with women who were convalescences, whom he loved in payment, nursing their dreams out of nightmare, helping them "actualize," until they were strong enough to have children, and he would leave.

○

GIVE ME A TIRED WOMAN, NOT A BITTER ONE, a divorced magician without the wand of her body, whose compassion contours her, whose wisdoms exceed the clinical pose of timing, needs and Jungian homilies. Give me a slow woman who has had everything and picks me like a roadside flower where she'd invest the universe, because why not and besides I make neat conversation, drop poems out of the corner of my eye, and drown in nostalgia because it is the buoyancy of my heart, because she likes my soul's style, likes old movies, knows everything has been said and there's only new ways to contemplate a flower, because such prayers circle the earth and move mountains, and you are only here to listen to another prayer. To understand that thinking makes it so and I have fleshed babes in the air; a meta-physician, in short, is what I want, not a thinker, someone whose heart and mind have stopped right in the throat, like a lump of sentiment that warbles the song, the world like an activist in the heart, who wakes me only for singing, and not for straightening my tie.

○

THE WOMEN I KNOW WIPE YOUR BROW and whisper desire in your ear, whisper a child, tomorrow, a movie, a career; even as they mop your brow they ask you, when you are only good to lean on, they ask you for the world that tires you, the world she mops from your brow, she asks for. There is no peace but from the marble skirts, the mercy you stare, like hot lassos, the unrequested, like a cool homage, the mercy you get you are so grateful for, you could swim oceans in thanks for a moment in her arms. But with the lovers, only shrieks and desperate cries will still them out of themselves; they know bankruptcy when they skirt it, and the moment of poetry in their eyes between desire and compassion, you mull it like a marble in your mouth, before the resumption of their need.

o

YOU MISS THE DAUGHTERS, AND PLAYING HOUSE, adopted ig-
norance to give her pleasure, the humblings you took which were dis-
graces — infantilism, to make her needed — to give her father and
child — to go crazy with service as she worshipped her womb. I see
myself. Her womb. I who concealed my God-lust, under papers, after
hours, who parcelled it while she slept, so as not to offend her with
metaphysics. The temple of silence when I was not with her, the
room upstairs where I scraped numen from my skull, where I married
her to the night — these she hated. And yet I miss my daughter, my
queen, after her third child in years to come, her laughter, uncredited
in her hunger.

o

YOU MUST SUBJECT THE WILL, or it is taken from you and re-
aligned to harmonies. Your crude plotting wakes the damsel. She is
not yours alone. You must surrender yourself, and she is not a
woman. She is the ideal, the hologram of heart we stumble into with
prejudicial sighs and races. The worship mandate with rough incarna-
tions. You are the virgin to idealization, spectral as quanta, with eyes
for metaphor. You are terribly free to love anyone after the fifth
woman. Your love is fleshed, companionable, heaves like a child in an
exhausted body. You have given birth to yourself.

o

HE SCREAMED FOR THE SKY to be a coverlet, for flowers to flesh
themselves in conversation. With weak eyes, he asked to have his eyes
out, so he could befriend darkness and be with spiritual light. The
kind he exhausted himself on while living. His hands yelled for home,
no more the chimera of it in poems, lips and acts of faith. His poems
grew hoarse with justification for the prodigal. He pleaded with

everything to let him in, but he'd already been there; there was nothing to do but to become everything, like the illegitimate saints at the soup line. The only work he knew how to do was loving; and he couldn't lie to do it anymore.

o

SHE IS THE MARY, the stroke of gentleness, the vertebrae of grasses, the mother grown men whimper to, harboured from slews of defilation, travestied stations of romance. She is the second body undevised I rampage to from the unrecognizable, the hardened quester. She is the lilted angle of my head as I watch leaves after a rain-storm breeze, the caress I left in a closet of hurts, carried now like a scimitar to faith, in the hands of the tenth donor.

o

SHE LOOKS AT HIM WITH MARBLE EYES, he fleshes, fractures to idea, refleshes from the kind words to a boy he met. Maturation-childhood, his brain scuttling in between like a wheelbarrow on a tightrope. Occasionally, she looks up when good faith has seized him by the scruff of the cortex and the handhold of heart. Balanced outside time and space, their eyes meet and his bones rivet to the skin for one more day, or eon — he can't guess; he knows this, truly, only, the instant of infused charity, the between-ness, where he can't live, where there are no typewriters, ice cream trucks, and deadlines. He wants to be called back from the shower of birds, shrieks and forlorn growings to embrace; to be called back from the door as he goes out, her eyes branding his clavicle like a calling.

o

SHE IS THE MOTHER who would let him go so he'd come back willingly, his conscience tarting him like a cameo engraved in his brain. His mother, loaned in the flesh, without her honour priming his skin for servitude. She is the mother of self-sacrifice he would wear his feet out for, his hemispheres, his nodes, his holograms, the pedestal he would fall on spent with the carcass of another earthen angel, a wrestled couple he could whip into a dervish of flight. It was not women he could love, unless he'd missed one, he asked her marble eyes for women that could hold him to the earth, a sign that could pronounce his name, a calling to the incarnate, marriage, children whom he could write for, like a toolsman for his son's cradle.

It is not quantifiable,
this essence; it is the ultra-mundane,
not mondial; it is the supra-physical but not
above anything, it is inside and outside —
hierarchical since you walk upright and
don't slither amoebically.
Poetry will do, or fast transforms
of intuition; but if you want to be the base
and free-play, but if you want to be observed-
observer, angst will look like vitality,
desperation look like heroism, need look like love.
You may apparition yourself, discountenanced,
your meta-face pine for kisses, your meta-
narrative will be your lifetime, your fiction
will encase your bones.
        She is not quantifiable, this she-name,
this quintessence of your gentling; she is you and
not you. She is not on the pedestal; she is love
reflecting herself. She is that without which
you would kill yourself, she is your soul
unfabricated and donated; otherwise you guess your
alpha, you send humanoids of thought to find your
legend; otherwise the mystery crushes you, you scavenge
yourself for the hands that made you,
your love will excavate you.
        She is in your eyes, in the teardrop and
in it the helix of mercy, your rosary decoded into
prayer or mutants. she is the pity you could
show to armies of children, if they'd let you;
she is the singing in your arterial shriek,
your grave suspicion, your always unquantifiable
suspicion of your loveliness.

The maximization of your cognitive freedom
will not still you, will not draw Her
close,
the maximization of your cognitive freedom
will bring you to your knees, get you
praying to your right brain, bring you stonehenge,
tribalize;
the maximization of your cognitive freedom will
Godify you, observed observer, etch your tablets
of cortical gelatin, sink them, raise them, redeem you
every five milliseconds, oscillating the heart to
shatter; the maximization of your cognitive freedom
will collar the spatio-temporal,
confess you, collapse, be built again;
busy ·hominoid, self-organizing nova with skin,
the maximization of your cognitive freedom
starves birds, water-colour etchings, holidays
from you;
the maximization of your cognitive freedom
is a nebula; your negentropy is on earth
like a ghost with a maypole.
When you are in two places at once
the quantum matrix of your body distends,
shedding the skin, lover; the meta-kiss is with
you in the paradigm of your self; remembered flesh
burns in you like a soul.
The maximization of your cognitive freedom
will bring you to mercy, demystify water
when the brain vapourizes,
when the terrestrial thirsts.

I AM TWO PERSONS. One does not know of the other. One knows
the maps, and has never travelled. The other has kept still, always,
has known the heart of the earth. The clamorous one has wasted
his time; the other is patient, lives in adoration, a single praising
heart, hands poetry to the other. The clamorous one must live
with his body, rues it, primes it. The heartful one lugs the body
with him like a father holding a child at a carnival.

How shall I absorb you,
take you in from the rain,   marry you to my skin,
you in the tenement
of my brain, you who waste yourself with
curing rafters. How shall I blot the anger from your
eyes, unfever your poems.
This is all I know of you. Perhaps that is why you do not
read your poems well, feeling yourself like braille.
I glimpse you when you are most fickle, rising like an exhumed
      ghost
from us, for I am the flesh and you are the code, the metaphor
      you
tell about. You are the gasp that interrupts us, the weak
lung; you see daylight and you position things.
There are glass bowls with falling snow.
Painted sets. A known universe, shrinking,
all ambitions had; you have known love and
desired me; you fall on me, fatigued, sincere
and begin to live, an extension of true life. You are
      mortality,

and you will hunt these words like sodden love letters,
hungry for the bread you make.
　　　I come out of your tears like a foal from her mother,
with such young lungs, like a memory of flight.
Try and remember you are not alone in this;
there are others born every day in the light
you shield from your eyes.

"If only men's minds could be seized and held still! They would see how eternity in which there is neither past nor future, determines both past and future time."
— St. Augustine

BEYOND THE CHILDISHNESS of solace and fear, the refuge of escape, there is the omni-modal prescience, the heart and mind conjunctive to the spirit, the body-spirit interface where God's eyelid closes, and you wish to open your body hypnotically to calling, where destiny is cinematic, and your next move purposeful, if not pre-visioned, and you must stop there and not presume your future. You melt the facts of your life to will, which is half yours and not yours, which does not bear much thinking, for the paradox is not yours to solve, but to contemplate. You live your life or rest. Nothing fanciful. You sing to your brother, the dawn, with his words, the way prayer is God's address to himself, your poems are what colours would say, what trees are. They say only one beauty, proper to their place and time. There is one objective moment in which the world knows itself. The poem is witness. It is not replicable, deducible or validated but in a smile in 1993 which conjures a branch in 1947. Acausally, trans-temporally across the avatars of mystery, through the jumble of parallel worlds, behind the wood of quantum volition, where the mind's scalpel burns, the heart arterializes the air, which is not ether, or stratosphere, or biosphere or noösphere, but acknowledged transcendence, a string to a finger, a word, a borrowed message, the unexpected kindness — the Sign, undecipherable and referring only to faith. Here is your intelligence, to speak for things as they appear on the chimera of time. Impatience will kill you. To know more is death. You will pray when you cannot listen.

ROSA NOVA
A MODERN PRAYER

Through intra-meditative resonances
            the rose occurs.
Through multi-spheric hierarchies from mote
            to ether
            the rose occurs.
Through sub-temporal bivouacs of dream, between
            trans-neural spasms and epiphanic interfaces,
            from the radial, luminal plasma of
            hands in prayer to the vernal codal waterfalls
            of bark the rose is apparitioned,
actually, invisibly, in the space between matter
            the cathedral is built, fleshing the intra-
phonemal purposefully, willing liaisons, carcassing earth to
sky, knotting the gurgle to the statesman's basso.
The rose, the aggregate of existential, the popular vote
            the supra-existential like a ghost behind
            the lining, the rose of your childhood,
extant after the canyons of cortical promise,
            recumbent, beauteous, the surprise
after the unnatural, the embalmings, the embryonic postures
            of mantra and microscope — you have the
            Rose;
salutant, primate, questor, in spite of everything
            the concomitant is with you, the blessing,
            the nitrate kiss of midnight
splicing the squealing engrams of your greed; the
            kiss softens you, an ineffable mother
            protracts your glare, cups your coronary
            fury, sends it to graze.

Thank you for the peace
I had known, refurbished
in the diademic cortex, above
the splintered crosses, the sour
cloud, thank you for hope, for the
word, Latinate on a heap of boards
in a Montreal laneway, a scrub's branch
on which I hung an Italian
word, gentleness, said "cielo, mano,
aria di nuovo" and packed my body
into them for cellular miracles,
came back on a train, unangered
with language, a sufficiency;
thank you for a Christmas, a home,
a skin of innocence, the magnetized
hand in grace, the old words dyed in
blood, the unrandomized snowflakes;
spirit, thank you, the tears I
vouched as beauty, just your light;
spirit misnamed, thank you, this
gratitude, grazie, ora, this hour.

INDEX OF TITLES